Madness in the Mainstream

Second Edition

Mark Drolsbaugh

HANDWAVE PUBLICATIONS

Madness in the Mainstream

Copyright © 2015 by Mark Drolsbaugh
Handwave Publications

Previous edition copyrighted in 2013

Cover design and layout courtesy of
Yvonne Vermillion, Magic Graphix

Cover photo by Jaime Eustace-Tecklin

ISBN: 978-0-9657460-7-6

Library of Congress Control Number: 2014915008

Published by:
Handwave Publications
1121 N. Bethlehem Pike #60-134
Spring House, PA 19477

Website: www.handwavepublications.com

This book is dedicated to the late, great George Carlin. Carlin had this remarkable ability to make people laugh. At the same time, he also got us to question what's going on in this warped world we live in. I hope this book makes people laugh and question what's going on in the warped world of deaf education.

Acknowledgements

To my wife Melanie and our three kids—Darren, Brandon, and Lacey. They've endured yet another round of "Just one more minute, Daddy's almost done."

To Dennis Jones Jr. Over the years Dennis has greatly influenced the way I think and write. I'm a better person for knowing Dennis.

To Yvonne Vermillion at Magic Graphix. Her expertise in layout and design brings life to every book she touches.

To Jaime Eustace-Tecklin for another great cover photo.

To Patty McFadden, Ally Balsley, Gina Oliva, and Karen Putz. Several ideas were bounced off of them when this book was in the beginning stages. Their encouragement kept me going during the times when I thought this would never get done.

One more acknowledgement goes to Darren. Seeing him deal with the challenges of the mainstream—and responding to them like the fighter he is—motivated me to say what had to be said.

Contents

Foreword

Mark Drolsbaugh is someone I've known for the better part of two decades. Not that I don't want to smack him sometimes. He's terrible about answering emails (though I have to admit he's gotten a little better). He knows this. I suspect somewhere deep inside, he does it on purpose so he can maintain his aura of eccentricity. He's also on what he calls a digital detox kick.

He's a writer. He has a self-deprecating sense of humor and is far too modest about his talents. I wish he'd knock the modesty off. He's more apt to make some sort of joke about how he's contributing to the degeneration of the American educational system than recognize his own abilities.

Talent like his is a gift. It's a gift I'm jealous of and covet. I daresay through his writings, he's gotten more people to think about the issues that really matter. If there's anyone who can convince people to clear the cobwebs out of their minds and think, for crissakes!, it's him.

What is especially aggravating is he can't write fast enough to satisfy me—he has *conviction*. Whatever he writes or says, he believes. It's laid bare for the world to take or leave.

1

As potent as this quality of his is, the one I find most admirable is his willingness to let people be who they are. He may disagree but he respects a person's right to decide their own path. 'Tis a good way to be, I think.

Of course, being the guy he is, he's got a repertoire of cuss words and dirty jokes he freely utilizes whenever we're together. This only adds to his charm.

Enjoy.

—Dennis Jones Jr.

Introduction

Aguest speaker from the Pennsylvania Department of Education opened his presentation with an obligatory mission statement. He clicked on the remote and immediately my colleagues and I—the only deaf people in attendance—let out a collective groan. There it was onscreen:

PDE's Commitment to Least Restrictive Environment

Our goal for each child is to ensure Individualized Education Program (IEP) teams begin with the general education setting with the use of Supplementary Aids and Services before considering a more restrictive environment.

Don't get me wrong. The Individuals with Disabilities Education Act (IDEA) guarantees an education to kids who otherwise might have been denied such an opportunity in the past. That's very commendable.

It's just that for some kids, especially deaf kids, a school district's interpretation of *Least Restrictive Environment* can do more harm than good. As you can see in PDE's statement above, the general education setting is

3

considered ideal while a classroom with people who have a lot in common with you is considered restrictive.

For an interesting contrast, here's an excerpt courtesy of the December 8, 2008 issue of *Sports Illustrated:*

They don't know other kids like themselves. But you put them in a world where there are other kids like them, and their self-esteem and all those other things that are hidden come out. You see them bloom.

This powerful quote came from an article titled *Unusual Direction* by Jack McCallum. It had nothing to do with deaf children. It was an article about kids with intellectual disabilities. But still, it applies to deaf children and anyone else who is different from mainstream society. And by "different," I'm not singling out people with disabilities. I'm talking about diverse groups of people all across the board who naturally benefit from interaction with their peers and role models.

I wouldn't want to be the only African-American in an all-white school. I wouldn't want to be the only boy in an all-girls school. I wouldn't want to be the only Jewish guy in a Catholic school. You get my drift. Being *The Only One* can be a painfully isolating experience. And yet this is what the interpretation of Least Restrictive Environment strives for if you're a deaf child.

If you can fit in with all of the hearing kids, congratulations! You're practically normal!

As of this writing, the economy is in the toilet and resulting budget cuts continue to threaten deaf schools and programs all over the country. Several have closed and others fight for their survival in the political arena every year. For better and for worse, mainstreaming continues to be the favored option for deaf children.

I made it in the mainstream. I've always said that if I wrote a book titled *I Made it in the Mainstream and Your Deaf Child Can, Too*, I'd be a millionaire by now. But there are some funny things that go on when a deaf guy tries to make it through the mainstream, regardless of whether he succeeds or not. A lot of these things fly under the radar.

The stories in this book give a unique perspective of life in the mainstream for deaf and hard of hearing students. Some of these stories were held out of my first book, *Deaf Again*, because I thought they were too inappropriate. *Deaf Again* was meant to be inspiring reading for people of all ages, so I tried to keep it clean. This time around, *Madness in the Mainstream* has material that would make Howard Stern blush.

Most of the stories in here aren't sob stories. Some of them are funny. I have no problem poking fun at myself because if we can laugh together, we can learn together.

Other stories are a bit heavier. If you're deaf or are close to someone who is, expect to get up and pace the room while muttering *dammit, I've got to do something about this.*

By the way, there's one more twist. This time around I'm writing as the father of a deaf kid. He's a mainstream success, too. His teachers are awesome. No problem with them at all. Likewise for his school district. They've provided everything my wife and I have asked for.

But the truth is: No matter how well you protect a deaf child in the mainstream from falling through the cracks academically, there are other cracks that inevitably appear. You'll find them in this book. And even though accessibility has improved a thousand-fold these days, my deaf kid still has to deal with the very same issues that turned me into a mental case when I was his age.

Dammit, I've got to do something about this.

Part I
Madness

The Lost Years

There's a period of my life that I often refer to as the lost years. From 1984 to 1989, I wandered aimlessly through the hearing world. This is the empty existence I often remind everyone about whenever there's a discussion on the long-term effects of mainstreaming.

It didn't matter that I graduated from Germantown Friends School, arguably one of the best high schools in the country. Academically I did fine. An American Sign Language (ASL) interpreter made sure of that. But socially? I was a mess.

There are some funny things that go on in your head when you're the only deaf kid in the entire school. First, you get used to being left out. It's like being a wallflower in training. You make the most out of whatever academic content you absorb and then you go home. You don't really get close to anyone, and even if you do, it's in small numbers. Large groups? Forget about it. Opportunities to jump into group discussions or demonstrate leadership skills are practically nil. How can you lead when you're too busy trying to keep up?

Second, the lack of deaf role models has a significant impact on a mainstreamed student's self-perception. Many deaf people, myself included, have made comments

9

about not believing in themselves or having lofty career ambitions until after they met successful deaf role models.

Nothing proves this more than my on-and-off college experience at Temple University. I enrolled at Temple in 1984 as an accounting major and had no idea what I was doing. The whole time I flunked accounting and economics ("If money's so tight, why don't they just print more of it?") I worked part-time at a local supermarket.

Deep down inside, I thought the supermarket job was as far as I'd ever go. The mantra *not bad for a deaf guy* often ran through my head as I stocked the shelves. Then I'd go out and party with my hearing friends.

"Party" meant getting rip-roaring drunk. As my childhood friends got older, that meant less playing on the ball field and more socializing in nightclubs. And socializing is a hell of a challenge if you're the only deaf person in the room.

First of all, an interpreter doesn't follow you around in the real world after you graduate. On top of that, my hearing friends didn't sign much (if at all). Nonetheless, these guys were still my childhood buddies. I love them. And I followed them into as many nightclubs and college parties as I could, like a loyal puppy. A puppy that always had one too many beers because he couldn't understand what anyone was saying.

Let's jump to 1987. There was this dorm party at Temple University. I didn't live in the dorm—I was a commuter student—so there was some security protocol that I had to follow in order to be allowed into the dorm on weekends. A student who lived in the dorm had to sign me in as a guest, and I had to turn in my student ID as collateral.

Once the party started I hung out with a mix of old childhood friends and some newer acquaintances from Temple. One of them, Vicky Mitchell, was a Temple

10

student who had a connection to Gallaudet University. In an ironic twist, she would later help me transfer to the place where I truly belonged.

But as for this particular evening, there was no such thing as belonging. I was a wallflower again. People chatted, laughed, and played party games. I smiled like an idiot.

All was not lost, however. I was an idiot with a *plan*. There was this other student, Alicia, who happened to be a gorgeous woman with a sweet personality. She really seemed to like me and was a fun person to be with. She didn't sign at all, which kind of slowed our communication down. But hey, she gave me the time of the day. That was a lot more than just about everyone else. So I couldn't help but wonder: *Is she the one?*

Self-doubt crept into my mind. What if Alicia was way out of my league? What if our friendship was ruined if I tried to take things to a level she wasn't interested in? Or, what if she was interested, and then I screwed it up with too much "Eh? What did you say?"

Can you believe this? I actually have a moral compass. No love life whatsoever and I'm worried about wrecking a platonic friendship.

So there I was, looking at Alicia and wondering if I should ask her out or not.

Did I mention she was a cheerleader? Definitely out of my league.

This soap opera took a strange turn when another woman entered the picture. Out of nowhere popped Kim, an obvious party animal. She had tattered blue jeans and a Guns 'n Roses t-shirt. Plain, stringy dirty blonde hair ran down her shoulders. She looked like a biker chick straight out of the '70s. Not drop-dead gorgeous like Alicia, but a nice figure and a sexy attitude. And...

Holy shit, she signs! Fluently!

11

What were the odds of this happening? Kim had a relative who was deaf, and as a result she had immersed herself in ASL at a very young age. She signed so fluently she looked deaf herself.

For those of you who are keeping score, here's the dilemma: A gorgeous cheerleader with a super personality... or a grungy, kinda sexy, but off-the-wall rock 'n roller who signs fluently.

I looked at Alicia. She looked back at me with those beautiful, sexy cheerleader eyes.

I looked at Kim. She burped and reached for another beer.

Eh. Alicia had the advantage based on familiarity and time spent together. But I didn't want to mess up our friendship.

My moral compass is strong, isn't it?

Kim sauntered up and put her arm around me.

"Want to party tonight?" she purred.

Out the window goes the moral compass. I'm getting some action, baby!

I told Alicia I'd catch up with her later. Kim and I went to another party somewhere upstairs. We got along beautifully. For once, it was a level playing field. I was having a bona fide conversation with... a woman! Who'da thunk it?

Oh, was I ever excited. But soon a different air of doubt clouded my mind. It wasn't self-doubt. It came from my friends. They'd seen me chatting with Kim and, for whatever reason, felt the need to do an intervention.

First it was Chuck, a guy from my economics class. He pulled me aside as I walked to the cooler for a drink.

"Dude," he said. "Watch what you're doing."

"Say what?"

"That girl you're with." Chuck made a circular motion around his ear. "She's nuts."

12

"That makes the two of us," I shrugged.

"No, man, I mean really. She's fucking nuts. She'll bite you. She will really, really bite you."

If you have any common sense, and I don't, you might recognize this as something we call a "red flag."

Nuts or not, this girl could *communicate*. I grabbed two beers and went back to Kim. As we continued chatting it up, another acquaintance of mine subtly sneaked up behind her. Without voicing, he slowly mouthed "Noooooooo!" while shaking his head and doing a cut-throat gesture.

That's two red flags right there.

It wasn't long before Kim and I needed another drink. Back to the cooler I went. And once more, someone tried to sabotage my romantic endeavors.

"Mark, you've got to trust me," said Steve, another Temple student. "She's psycho." Steve slowed down his speech so that there would be no doubt what he was saying. "She's... going... to... bite... you. Bail... out."

As if that warning wasn't enough, there was a guy pantomiming right behind Steve. He pointed at Kim, bit on his index finger, crossed his eyes in pain and mouthed "Owwww."

Three red flags. And you have to give my buddies credit. They might not know sign language, but their visual-gestural communication skills are off the charts.

I made my way back to my seat and handed Kim another drink. She smiled and moved closer to me. Our conversation went on. I can tell you without a doubt that in just thirty minutes, I talked to Kim a lot more than I talked to any other woman on campus in the past two years.

Meanwhile, my friends were relentless. They continued making cut-throat gestures, mouthing the word "no," and biting their fingers for emphasis. They seemed to be genuinely concerned about my wellbeing. I gave them the

13

thumbs-up to let them know I had the situation under control.

At that point I noticed Kim had absolutely inhaled another drink. I'd barely taken two sips from mine and she was already done.

"Want another drink?" I offered.

And then it happened.

Kim turned pale. Or was it green? Either way, she was ready to hurl.

A trash can probably would have come in handy. But Kim didn't need one. She nonchalantly reached for her empty beer bottle and—

Hooo-wwworrrfffff!

She vomited into the bottle. All of it, without yarking on her shoes or anything. I was amazed how she managed to unload all of her barf into such a small opening. Obviously she'd done this before, because she gently put the bottle down and went on with our conversation as if nothing happened.

If that isn't a red flag, I don't know what is.

Let me admit that for a nanosecond—just for a nanosecond—I was thoroughly grossed out. But as soon as she put the bottle down, Kim went back to being Potential Girlfriend Who Knows ASL. Who else in the dorm could communicate with me on that level? All I could see was a great opportunity. So continue to hang out with Ms. Bottle Barfer, I certainly did.

"Would you like to come with me to my room?" she winked. I smiled affirmatively.

We made our way back to her room and it wasn't long before we were wrapped in a passionate embrace. As we gently kissed, the thought never crossed my mind that ten minutes ago, those succulent lips were heaving into a beer bottle.

Am I an idiot or what?

"Let me put some music on," Kim signed, swaying back and forth. "I want to dance with you."

Nice!

Of course, she put on a punk rock album that woke up half the dorm. She didn't care. She just grabbed me and started slow dancing.

How you slow dance to the Sex Pistols, I don't know, but slow dance we did. Why not? Whatever floats her boat.

I was doing pretty well when all of a sudden Kim grabbed me by the head with both hands. Her fingernails damn near dug into my scalp. She pulled me closer and screamed into my face.

"CAN YOU HEAR THE MUSIC?"

Whoa. I backed away and said, yes, I could hear it well enough. She grabbed my head again.

"BULLSHIT!"

If you're keeping count, that's five red flags. What the hell am I doing in there?

I explained to her that yes, I really could hear the music, but just the instruments. I wasn't able to hear or understand the lyrics. That was enough for Ms. Bottle Barfer to grab me by the scalp again.

"YOU CAN HEAR! YOU CAN HEAR!" she barked. And then, suddenly switching gears—or was it personalities?—she gently put her arms around me and leaned forward. I puckered my lips in anticipation.

Her mouth missed mine. She kept going a little further south. Down my neck. Where she opened wide and started to dig in her teeth.

What part of "She will really, really bite you" did I not understand? Chuck, Steve, and all of those pantomiming idiots were truly looking out for my best interests. But mainstreaming had left me so starved for communication that I was eager to hook up with a vampire wannabe.

15

Finally, I came to my senses. I backed away, said a quick "See ya," and bolted down the hall. I zipped down the stairs in two bounds and headed for the main lobby. The only thing standing in the way of my escape from certain doom was a security guard at the front desk.

He wouldn't let me leave.

"Really, I gotta go," I pleaded.

"Sorry, can't do that," the guard insisted. "Dorm rules. I can't return your ID and you can't leave until the person who signed you in signs you out."

I scratched my head. I couldn't remember which one of my buddies signed me in. Even if I did, I had no idea where to find him. The parties were long since over. It was almost dawn.

"Look," I told the guard. "I thought I was staying overnight, okay? Then this girl tried to bite me, and—"

"Oh, you were with Kim!" the guard grinned. He chuckled, handed over my ID, and motioned for me to be on my way. I thanked him and hopped out of there as fast as I could.

Welcome to the Madness in the Mainstream. Read on and find out how it got to be that way.

Out of Order

Deaf children are almost always placed in hearing schools first. They're gradually sifted through a series of options (including assistive technology, itinerant teachers, interpreters, self-contained classrooms, and so on) until they arrive at something that works.

Notice how they start with auditory-based options and then move on to visual, deaf-friendly options later, only if necessary? For the kids who are visual learners, a lot of valuable learning time is lost.

Over the years I've walked a fine line when writing about this. After all, I've interned and worked at deaf schools for more than two decades. This didn't stop me from writing articles such as *ASL: Not Guilty* and *ASL is a Bridge, Not a Barrier* in the anthology *Anything But Silent*. But there was a clear sense that I was pushing limits, and there were times when I was asked to choose my words carefully.

Watch what you say, be careful, stay neutral, don't bite the hand that feeds you, don't upset the politicians who control the funding, just be a good boy and sit in the corner over there.

It's different now. I write this book not as an employee of a particular school. My opinions and beliefs do not necessarily reflect those of anyone I've worked with or am working with now.

I write this book as a deaf adult who is now the parent of a deaf child. In this role, the gloves are off. How can they not be? I want what's best for my kids. The only way to ensure this is to speak my mind as soon as possible. No time for *train gone*.

I hate to be cynical. But things long ago reached the point where anytime a deaf student was referred out of his or her school district and into a school for the deaf, I could only say three words:

What's the catch?

I'm reluctant to reveal this because in my heart, I believe that each and every child has a right to the most accessible, appropriate education. It's just that the timing—the matter of when (and where) they get that education—is often out of whack.

Perhaps the best way to blow this topic out the water is to rehash an actual conversation I had with my wife, Melanie.

Mark: Ever notice how every time a deaf kid is transferred to a deaf school, there's a lot of baggage attached?

Melanie: Academically or developmentally delayed, right?

Mark: Yeah. They're either significantly delayed or have behavior issues. Or both.

Melanie: Nothing new.

Mark: I know. But I have a question. I think I have a new perspective.

Melanie: I told you, it's nothing new. Deaf schools are almost always offered as a last resort. Parents should be given the option of selecting deaf schools first instead of having it at the end of a checklist.

Mark: Yeah, I know, but it's not just that. I just realized something else. Remember Joey? (Name changed for confidentiality)

Melanie: Yeah. Same situation.

Mark: Right. But his school district knew he was deaf two years before they sent him to a deaf school. So at the time he was identified as deaf, he could have been placed in a deaf school. But no, they put him in a hearing school.

Melanie: Like I said, nothing new. Fail at a hearing school first and then go to a deaf school. Wastes a lot of time.

Mark: I know. But look at it this way. Obviously his being deaf had nothing to do with his being placed in a deaf school.

Melanie: Yes it did. They just exhausted the other options first.

Mark: Maybe, but wait a second. A deaf school was never an option until after they realized he had significant social-emotional issues.

Melanie: They don't know what else to do.

Mark: Maybe. But look. He was sent to a deaf school not because he was deaf. If it was because he was deaf, he would have been sent there two years ago. But they sent him to a deaf school almost immediately after it was determined he couldn't function in the mainstream due to a condition that has nothing to do with deafness.

Melanie: They'll never admit that. They'll say deafness is primary.

Mark: And we both know that's a flat-out lie. If deafness was primary then they just wasted two years of this kid's life. So now we've established that he was sent to a deaf school because of his behavior problem.

Melanie: Like I said, nothing new.

Mark: Yeah, yeah. But there's more strange thinking behind this. Look at it this way: He was sent to a deaf school because of his behavior, all right? Now look at the staff at the deaf school. Is there anyone there with sufficient training to handle that?

Melanie: (Smirks)

Mark: Seriously. Does anyone at the deaf school have the training to deal with the wide range of social-emotional and behavioral issues that Joey has?

Melanie: Of course not.

Mark: Then why send a kid to a deaf school because of significant social-emotional and behavioral issues if the staff at that school has little or no training in those areas? If Joey wasn't deaf, he'd be in a residential treatment facility by now.

Melanie: Are you done venting? I told you this is nothing new.

Mark: I know, I know. But I'm onto something. Now tell me real quick: What do the teachers at the deaf school have that the teachers at the hearing school don't have? Don't tell me "expertise in behavioral disorders" because in general that's not true. What do the teachers at the deaf school have that the teachers at the hearing school don't have?

Melanie: Communication skills.

Mark: More specifically?

Melanie: The deaf school is loaded with staff fluent in ASL. It's a more communicatively accessible environment.

Mark: Damn right. So when the school district needs a miracle worker, they depend on ASL to rescue everyone.

Melanie: Sometimes it works.

Mark: Definitely. Remember Steve, Jessica, Michael, and Tommy? (Names changed for confidentiality)

Melanie: Yes. They did great.

Mark: And they were at our school not because they were deaf, but because they were autistic. Michael wasn't even deaf. Did you see the difference ASL made in their lives? They were lost souls when they came in. They were full of life when they left. Steve kicked ass in a school play, remember?

Melanie: Yes, I remember that. But that group was different. They didn't really have any behavior problems. They were just autistic. Are you saying deaf schools should reject special needs kids?

Mark: No, not at all. That group rocked. What I'm saying is, the door was wide open for them. That's fine. But that same door slams shut for most of the other deaf kids who deserve an opportunity to go to a deaf school.

Melanie: Maybe the school district looks at deaf schools solely as a therapeutic placement.

Mark: Yeah. That pisses me off. A deaf school is a place where deaf kids learn—normally!—through a different

21

language. ASL has broken down barriers for so many kids and the school district knows this. They know how much of an impact ASL has. And they still withhold it until the last possible second. If they know it's so effective, why hold it back?

Melanie: Like I said, ASL should be offered fairly as a possible first option instead of last.

Mark: And it's not! It would be one thing if they didn't know anything about ASL. But they *know* it works and they still hold it back. I'm telling you, that's clearly audism. They value the ears and the mouth so much that they won't go to the hands—hands that *work*—unless they have no other choice.

Melanie: I know. It's sad. Are you finished?

Mark: Hell, no! I'm just getting started.

Melanie: (groans)

Mark: I know you hate it when I rant like this. But look, the school district's logic goes totally downhill from there. Let me review one more time: They know that ASL is effective. When the chips are down and they have unresponsive kids with multiple issues that they can't handle, that's when they decide an ASL-friendly deaf school will save the day.

Melanie: Right. Nothing new. How many times do I have to say "nothing new?"

Mark: Hold on, it gets better. Now look at it this way: If they think ASL is such a miracle for all of the kids with this, this, and that... why don't they go ahead and make the most of it for all of the regular deaf kids out there who need it too? What I just said about the door

22

slamming shut for them is similar to what Amy Cohen Efron said in her *Greatest Irony* vlog. She explained how hearing parents are busting down doors to teach hearing babies ASL, while deaf babies are forbidden from using it. This is an extension of the same thing!

Melanie: Yes, I see your point.

Mark: Thank you. So again, why are so many deaf kids... who stand to benefit so much from the language accessibility deaf schools provide... denied the opportunity until it's way too late?

Melanie: I know, I know...

Mark: Audism. I rest my case.

Welcome to the Mainstream

In *Deaf Again,* I described my elementary school years at Plymouth Meeting Friends School as the calm before the storm. PMFS is a small K-6 Quaker school where my deafness rarely caused any problems.

First and foremost, I was not yet profoundly deaf. I was still in the early stages of a progressive hearing loss and thus was able to keep up with small group discussions. Since PMFS is a small private school, pretty much every discussion was a small group discussion. The staff to student ratio of 1:4 often worked to my advantage.

The close-knit environment at PMFS helped me get used to each student's speech pattern to the point where one-on-one conversations were relatively easy. In fact, I was even able to talk on the phone with some of my more patient classmates. My best friend Norman, for example, often spelled out words that I couldn't understand on the phone.

"Jenny told Trisha she thinks you're cute. Cute. I said, CUTE! C-U-T-E! No, I didn't say you're cute. What kind of a question is that? Jenny said you're cute. JENNY! J-E-N-N-Y!"

Then there was the issue of social skills. In elementary school you don't really need to be a master

24

conversationalist. Social time at recess is mostly kickball, dodgeball, tag, or any other game. If you knew how to take turns and get through a game without arguing, you were part of the In Crowd.

Junior high school is an entirely different animal.

My family enrolled me at Germantown Friends School for the seventh grade. It soon became obvious that communication was going to be a huge challenge. Not only was the student body at GFS much larger than what I was used to at PMFS, but my hearing loss continued to get worse.

GFS recognizes that the transition from elementary school to junior high is a big one. For this reason they have an annual seventh grade camping trip right before the beginning of the school year. They believe that a couple days of community-building activities allow everyone to bond and get off to a good start. Unfortunately, a good start for the hearing kids can be a traumatic one for the lone deaf kid.

When I was dropped off at the GFS parking lot, there were over one hundred seventh graders milling around. This was almost ten times as many students I graduated with at PMFS. Right off the bat, I was lost.

There were maybe four or five kids I knew from little league. I swapped a quick how-do-ya-do with each of them. Sure, I could play with them for two hours on a baseball field, but a two-hour bus ride was another story. I didn't say another word to anyone as I sat silently by the window.

Fast-forward for a second here. If you ask any of my old Gallaudet University baseball teammates, they'll tell you I couldn't shut up on the team bus. Our road trips had plenty of stories and jokes and I was involved in most of them. It's like night and day when you compare trips with deaf and hearing peers.

25

As the buses arrived at the campgrounds, I grabbed my stuff and played the old game of *figure out where I'm going.* As various GFS staff announced who needed to go where for what activity, I had to corner them afterwards to remind them I was deaf.

In some mainstream programs this is lauded as "having excellent self-advocacy skills." Fuck that. My anxiety level was off the charts.

Soon I figured out which group I was assigned to and followed what they were doing the best that I could. Unlike at PMFS, I could not understand a word anyone said.

Time to go into survival mode.

During the team-building activities, I got into the habit of making sure I stayed near the end of the line. This way I was able to buy enough time to figure out what we were doing. By the time it was my turn, it looked like I was an old pro. Some of the staff actually thought I was able to follow their directives. Until...

"Mark, stay off the asphalt."

As we walked down the road towards the next team-building activity, our staff leader wanted to make sure we stayed off to the side in case there was any oncoming traffic. It took me a while to figure this out.

"Huh?"

Was he talking to me?

"Mark, I said stay off the asphalt."

Shit. He's definitely talking to me. And everyone's staring.

"Huh?"

This was embarrassing. Could it possibly get any worse?

Yes, it could.

One of those kids who played in my baseball rec league realized what was going on. He moved closer to me so I could read his lips.

"He said stay off the asphalt."

"Huh? Wave off my ass fart?"

Welcome to junior high, kid.

Later that evening the whole seventh grade gathered together in a large cabin. A staff leader barked out directions, and once again I just stood there without a clue while several students broke off into small groups. They huddled in small circles and apparently they were planning something. Was it some kind of competition? A scavenger hunt? Ghost stories? Who knew?

As far as I could tell, whatever activity was going on must have been an optional one. Some of the students stayed seated where they were. I moved towards the back of the room and sat behind them.

One by one, each group took turns performing an improvisational skit. I sat there bored out of my mind. Time slowed down to an agonizing eternity.

Uh-oh. The staff leader is looking at me again. What does he want now?

Apparently the skits were pretty good and the staff decided everyone should get involved. I could see the staff leader pointing towards kids in the back and calling them out. My heart skipped a beat when he briefly made eye contact with me. As discreetly as possible, I moved to the other side of the room. Damned if I was going to let him put me in a position where I'd make a total ass out of myself on stage.

Let's fast-forward again. At an all-deaf Halloween party in 2002, my good buddy Neil McDevitt—dressed up as improv comic and sitcom star Drew Carey— decided to initiate a game based on Carey's popular Whose Line Is It Anyway? *television show. Several people immediately nominated me as one of the contestants. I did not disappoint. During the "Scenes from a Hat" segment, I was assigned the role of "President of*

Gallaudet University on crack." What followed was an improv commencement address that had everyone howling with laughter. See what I'm getting at? Night and day.

There had to be a way out of this mess. I glanced around in desperation and found the exit. Standing in front of the door—and my escape from Hearing People Hell—was another staff leader. It was Caroline, my soon-to-be history teacher. I'd managed to establish a friendly rapport with her earlier in the day. Perhaps if I talked to her, she'd understand.

"Uh, Caroline?" I stammered.

"Yes, Mark?"

"I twisted my ankle today and it's really bothering me. Mind if I go back to the campground and lie down?"

Was that a lame-ass excuse or what?

At first Caroline glanced across the room, apparently looking for whoever had the first aid kit. It would only take a couple of minutes to wrap my allegedly sore ankle. But then Caroline stopped and looked me in the eye.

"Are you sure?"

Caroline wasn't stupid. She knew exactly what was going on.

"Yeah. I just need to rest up. I'll be fine."

"Okay, go ahead. Good night, Mark."

I thanked Caroline and headed back to the campground, where I curled up in my sleeping bag and gazed at the stars.

I breathed a sigh of relief. The stars were much better company than anyone in the cabin. At that moment I might have been alone, but at least I was no longer lonely. That's just the way it is.

This was a huge turning point in my life. It was right there in that sleeping bag, lying alone under the stars, when I realized that I was on my own. As long as I allowed other people to make decisions for me, my life was going to be a living hell.

And this is precisely why I cringe every time someone insists that mainstream schools are the Least Restrictive Environment.

Mainstreaming vs. Deaf School: A Baseball Version

While grown-ups everywhere argue about the pros and cons of mainstreaming for deaf children, we often forget to seek input from the real experts.

Who's that, you ask?

The very kids who go through it, of course.

Real-life experience beats professional opinion and educational policy every time. Research can be twisted to show what people want it to show. School districts can thump their chests and insist they know a Least Restrictive Environment when they see one. More often than not, money and politics overrule common sense.

But children are brutally honest. If you really want to know the truth, then all you have to do is just ask. Ask with an open mind and you'll get an open-minded answer.

I bring this up because my son Darren gave me a whopper of a reality check. Even I, Mr. Deaf Dad, can sometimes overlook the truth behind a deaf child's experience. All the more reason to pay attention to what our kids are saying.

Editor's note: You're going to see a lot of Darren in this book. Most of his experiences in here occurred between

30

the ages of nine and fourteen. For the most part he's a mainstream success. But when he vents about certain things, it clearly shows we're way overdue for a book like this.

Darren is nine years old as of this writing. His two main passions are baseball and art. I don't know much about art other than I think it's a healthy outlet for kids. So let's focus on baseball.

Darren is a helluva ballplayer. He's got remarkable control for a pitcher his age. He also has an uncanny changeup that he can use effectively during games. Defensively, he's a whiz at shortstop and third base. He's made some highlight-reel catches that you wouldn't believe. Offensively, he's a solid hitter who rips a lot of doubles and triples.

Obviously I'm a proud dad. But what I'm most proud of is Darren's spirit. One time he was up at bat with the bases loaded in a close game, and he got hit by a pitch in the rear end. He promptly hopped up, ran to first base, and high-fived the first base coach. The RBI meant more to him than the triple he hit a couple innings earlier. He took one for the team. I jokingly told him he earned a Run Butted In.

He hates that joke, by the way.

I decided to reward this kid's passion for baseball by signing him up for an exclusive, professional baseball camp hosted by none other than his heroes, the Philadelphia Phillies.

Yes, I signed him up for two weeks at the Phillies Baseball Academy. Two weeks of bona fide instruction, drills, and games under the tutelage of the very best in the business.

These guys are really good at what they do. They've got a perfect balance of learning and fun, and Darren had a great time during the daily intrasquad games. Among the highlights were a bases-loaded triple and a double play he turned while playing shortstop. He played with a lot of heart and proudly wore "gamer" pins on his baseball cap—pins that were awarded by Phillies' staff for his hustle and spirit.

I personally enjoyed visiting the camp to watch the games. When it was Darren's turn to pitch, *ziiiiip!* It looked like he added a couple of miles per hour on his fastball. Darren gleefully explained that the coach taught him how to improve his grip. He also learned the difference between a four-seam and a two-seam fastball.

Later, Darren fell behind 3-1 in the count and promptly threw two straight changeups. The batter swung at the first one and missed. The next one fluttered by for a called third strike. Darren hopped back to the bench with a big grin on his face. Again, the coach had helped him make some adjustments; he improved his changeup so much that he was able to throw it consistently for strikes, even in fastball counts such as 2-0 or 3-1.

Before we get to the part where I pull the rug out from everyone, I'd like to answer the inevitable question: "What the hell were you doing putting a deaf kid in an all-hearing camp?" The answer to that question is the fact that Darren is late-deafened. He's in that in-between world right now where he pretty much gets along well with both deaf and hearing kids. He really loves his rec league. Many of the players are from his school so he's comfortable playing with them. Last but not least, this kid is a rabid Phillies fan. To be able to play a number of games while wearing the uniform of the Philadelphia Phillies, I figured that would be baseball heaven right there.

Ready for the rug burn?

Every year the camp session culminates in a trip to Citizens Bank Park. The campers get to tour the stadium, walk on the field, meet one of the Phillies, and get their pictures taken. What a way to end the summer baseball season, eh?

Three weeks later, the pictures arrived.

YANK! There goes the rug.

A picture says a thousand words. It really does. So I'm standing there, looking at Darren's team picture, when I notice all of the kids have beaming smiles on their faces.

Except for Darren. He looked like he just came out of dentist's camp. He had a mostly emotionless expression, with a little hint of sadness.

Time to talk to the kid.

"Darren, come here for a minute. What did you think of Phillies camp?"

"It was good." (Shrugs)

"No, really. Tell me what you really thought about it. Fun? Boring? Awesome? Sucky?"

Notice how my parenting skills include words like "sucky"? Damn, I'm good.

Darren shrugged again. He knows I love the Phillies too. I got the sense he didn't want to let me down.

"Look," I said, bringing the picture to his attention. "This kid looks happy. That kid looks excited. The kid over here looks proud. And this kid looks so thrilled, he's peeing his pants."

The pee-your-pants joke gets them every time.

"All right," I continued. "Let's look at you. How are you feeling in that picture? It's okay, you can tell me."

"Sad."

"That's okay. It's good to be honest about how you're feeling. What made you feel sad that day?"

"I don't really know any of those kids."

"Hard to understand them?"

"Yes. It didn't feel good. I liked the games but didn't know the kids."

"You miss your real team, the Sea Wolves?"

33

"Yeah. I want to play Fall Ball with them."

"You got it. Look, you can be honest. Don't put yourself through something that's not comfortable for you. If you don't like something, you can tell us anytime."

"I love baseball. I love pitching. Just not there."

"That's okay. So are you saying you don't want Phillies camp next year?"

"Yeah. Just the Sea Wolves is enough."

Okay, that's enough of that classic father-son moment. Now I need to wrap up this piece by emphasizing three things:

1. The Phillies Academy is an *awesome* camp. I'll recommend that camp to anyone. Not only did they greatly improve Darren's pitching skills, but they also offered specific hitting and fielding instruction along with a remarkably accurate scouting report. Darren beams with pride and shows everyone this report. It means the world to him. You'll often find him in the backyard with his brother Brandon, working on the suggestions that the Phillies staff recommended. He and I are grateful for everything the Phillies have done for him.

2. A picture says a thousand words. Although Darren had fun here and there, for the most part he felt isolated in what was a mainstream environment. The team picture says it all. That moment is frozen in time and it allows a glimpse into Darren's soul. A soul that's crying *Get me out of here*. It's heart-wrenching, really. Which begs the question: *At least Darren still managed to have fun playing baseball in between the "boring hearing moments." But what about all those deaf kids stuck sitting in hearing classrooms all over the world?* I guarantee you that most of them feel the same way Darren did in that picture. They'll rarely tell you if you don't ask them.

3. The next camp Darren goes to, baseball or anything else, is going to be a deaf camp. There is simply no substitute for being around your real peers.

One more thing. Fast-forward two weeks later and there's Darren on a field playing softball. Some of the players on my softball team are having an informal practice before the start of our Fall Softball League. There aren't enough players for a real practice session; it's just a last minute what-the-heck-let's-hit-a-ball-around thing. Darren and Brandon joined us to help chase down some balls in the outfield.

Let me tell you, one look at Darren and you could see the spark was back in his eyes. Every player on the field was deaf. It was a level playing field, pardon the pun.

One player ripped a line drive to left field and Darren made a diving catch. That's the Darren I know. Dirty clothes, big grin on his face.

Towards the end of practice one of our best hitters started ripping balls out of the park. Darren went around the field to retrieve the homerun balls on the other side of the fence. He decided to stay there rather than waste time going back and forth. When the next ball flew over the fence, Darren caught it and raised his glove triumphantly.

Finally, practice was over. As a gesture of appreciation my team stayed on the field a bit longer to throw batting practice to Darren and Brandon. After Darren finished hitting, he took a quick run around the bases. A couple of my teammates playfully chased him after he passed second base. Responding to the challenge, Darren accelerated as he rounded third and slid into home plate.

Safe at home.

In more ways than one.

Speech vs. Resilience

Some people find it disturbing that I don't place much value on my speech ability. Not to disparage the speech teachers out there who are skilled at working with deaf children, but back in my day I had no integrated speech therapy. For me, speech meant getting pulled out of math class. When a classmate at Germantown Friends School noticed I was the last one to catch onto the quadratic formula, he asked me point blank:

"You missed all of this just so you could practice saying *she sells sea shells by the seashore?*"

"Yep," I confirmed. "But it was worth it. Look what I can do now: *She shat shitballs by the seashore. The shit she shat were shitballs I'm sure.*"

We laughed, but my friend was right. Speech might have been fun in grade school, where a really creative speech teacher helped me master those damned R's that often had me tongue-tied. But in junior high, there was no time to waste. Why should I spend any more time on the R's when my classmates were exploring the whole world of knowledge with the other twenty-five letters of the alphabet? I complained about this to my deaf parents and they agreed. They pulled the plug on my speech sessions and I was glad to be done with it.

It would be an understatement to say my hearing relatives were upset when they learned I dropped speech.

How could he not want speech? It's the basis behind all communication in the world as we know it!

I don't fuss over speech because it takes a lot more than that to succeed in this world. It takes knowledge and resilience. Speaking of resilience, I have a story that proves my point.

During the early 1980's, there was a significant technological change that had a major impact on my job. Back then I was a supermarket clerk who often worked the most insane hours, especially the graveyard shift on Saturdays. The reason behind this was we always had to scramble to make sure our price changes matched what was advertised in the Sunday papers.

This was back in the days when we used a label gun to stick prices onto each individual product. If the price went up for a certain item, we had to use a black marker to cross out the old price, and then we'd carefully place a new price sticker on top of it. Some of us used a specially-designed razor to remove the old sticker entirely. This covert operation was carried out in the wee hours of the morning so that no one would ever know we raised the prices.

If the price of an item was reduced, however, we were encouraged to be a little sloppy in the price-changing procedure. We'd cross out the old price with a transparent red marker, and affix the new price sticker right next to it. This way, our customers could compare prices and say *Hey! I saved thirty-seven cents!* Either way, we had to do this as fast as we could. Adding to the urgency was the store guarantee that if the wrong price was on an item, the customer got it for free.

You wouldn't believe how many old ladies with magnifying glasses came in. Every one of them was

37

a Sherlock Holmes wannabe. They were hell-bent on unlocking the mystery of the overpriced zucchini.

This system took up an inordinate amount of time. Fortunately, this changed when our store overhauled the checkout counters so that they could scan UPC barcodes. Can you imagine the time this saved? No more label guns. No more schlepping around with stickers. No more teams of employees working feverishly at ridiculous hours of the night to get this done on schedule. With the UPC system in place, all we needed to do was place one small plastic price card on the shelf. When a price change occurred, it only took one employee a few seconds to replace the card.

Up front at the checkout counters, the cashiers no longer had to search for price stickers and manually enter the numbers on the cash registers. All they had to do was zip the products over a scanner and the price was automatically rung up. Needless to say, the lines moved a lot faster.

This new technology was so efficient that it posed an entirely new problem. The time it saved added up to a lot of man-hours the company didn't know what to do with. Lines moved so quickly that they no longer needed a cashier manning every register; just a few cashiers were now able to do the work of many, and in a shorter amount of time.

The same problem applied to supermarket clerks. Pricing and price changes were now a piece of cake. Management was faced with the prospect of having to cut back hours, or even lay off staff entirely. And what were they going to do with the deaf kid in the general merchandise department?

"Uh, Mark," said Steve, the assistant general manager. "We're putting you in the pharmacy."

"You're putting him *where?*" interrupted Harry, my department manager.

38

"What else can we do?" said Steve. "There aren't enough hours on the floor. It's either the pharmacy or let him go."

Harry simmered, but I was fine with it. The pharmacy sounded cool. Until they told me what my job responsibilities were.

"You're putting me *where?*" I asked, repeating Harry's incredulous response.

"You'll be fine, Mark," Steve reassured me. "We know you can handle the front desk."

I scratched my head. The front desk of the pharmacy meant dealing directly with customers picking up their prescriptions. We also had a photo center, so a lot of people came in to pick up their pictures as well.

This didn't make sense. I was great at stocking shelves, taking inventory, and doing price changes. But my biggest weakness was dealing with customers. I had a hard time understanding most of them. They often asked for help with finding items in the store, which often led to a series of foul-ups, bleeps and blunders. And management was intentionally putting me in a position where I'd foul up on a regular basis? They were insane. Harry told them as much.

"Front desk at the pharmacy?" Harry fumed. "You have *got* to be kidding me. You don't put a deaf kid at the front desk. The hell are you thinking?"

"He'll be fine," Steve reiterated. "He speaks very well for a deaf person."

"His speech isn't the problem! It's when people talk back to him when he has no fucking idea what's going on!"

Harry's statement of the obvious meant nothing to Steve. So there I was the very next day, smiling like an idiot behind the counter at the pharmacy. Things got interesting right away.

"Good morning," I said, to the first customer who walked in. "How may I help you?"

My speech is very good!

"Good morning," the man smiled back. "I'd like to pdksl shdxp qwsdty ."

Shit! Harry was right. I had no fucking idea what was going on.

"Eh?" I mumbled, pointing to my ears. "I'm sorry, I'm deaf. Could you repeat that please?"

The customer left.

I smacked my head. This was the same thing that happened at my regular post in general merchandise. If I told customers that I was *deaf,* they often responded as if it was the Bubonic Plague. For whatever reason they reacted better when I just said I was a little hard of hearing.

As my very first customer made a hasty exit, Steve walked by and stopped for just a second. I could have sworn I saw a smirk on his face.

That son of a bitch, I thought to myself. *He actually wants me to screw up.*

Soon another customer walked in. This time it was a pleasant little old lady. Call me sexist, but it's been my experience that women are, by far, better communicators than men. I felt more confident this time.

"Good morning," I said, with my excellent speech. "How may I help you?"

"Good morning," the dear little old lady responded. "I need trsgp kdhfg swrtqs cdfsgly."

Once again, my excellent speech was worthless. In fact, the more I open my yap, the more everything falls apart. Hearing people often think that the better you speak, the better you can hear. There are deaf people I know who actually garble their speech on purpose so that hearing people will be sure to enunciate their words more clearly.

"Excuse me," I said, once again pointing to my ears. "I'm a bit hard of hearing. Could you repeat that please?"

"Oh, I'm sorry," the nice lady said, smiling and speaking slower. "I'm here to pick up a prescription."

Whew. So far, so good.

"No problem," I said. "And your name is?"

"Shdgfi Trwqxr."

Shit.

It was time to improvise. That's life, after all. If there's an obstacle, find a way around it. What else are you going to do?

C'mon, Drolz. Think. Figure something out.

"Just a moment, please," I smiled. "I'll be right back."

I rummaged through a supply shelf and found exactly what I needed. A clipboard, a blank piece of paper, and a pen. Bingo! An instant sign-in sheet.

"Sign your name right here, please," I asked the nice lady. She complied, and it was easy to find her prescription with that information.

Soon there was a line of customers and instead of playing verbal volleyball with the deaf guy, they just signed in and their orders were ready to go. I still had to do some lipreading, but that was narrowed down by simply asking customers if they were there to pick up prescriptions or photos. It's much easier to lipread when you know what to expect. There were occasional glitches, sure, but most of the time the line moved smoothly. And no matter what happened, I refused to look flustered. Why give anyone the satisfaction?

Sure enough, when Steve made his rounds again he stopped in front of the pharmacy and saw that I hadn't cracked. Some of the customers told him how inspiring it was when I refused to let my deafness get in the way. Steve gave me a blank look and walked off.

Yeah, go on, keep walking. I got a job to do.

A couple of weeks later I found myself back at my old position in general merchandise. Although the UPC system threw everyone off guard with its remarkable efficiency, it wasn't long before the brains behind the corporation figured out how to fill in the extra free time. More work went into expanding the store and that in turn created more jobs. This led to me going right back where I belonged.

As I resumed stocking shelves on my first day back, a fellow co-worker, Sue, stopped by to say hello.

"Welcome back," she smiled.

"Thanks," I replied. "I'm glad to be back. Things got kind of interesting in the pharmacy."

"You can say that again," Sue laughed. "But let me tell you something."

Sue was our store's union representative. She was small in stature, a woman in her thirties who stood something like five foot two. But she was tough both physically and in character. You could see the muscles rippling on her arms as she unloaded boxes in the back room. She stood up to anyone who gave her a hard time. And, as union rep, she stood up to management whenever necessary.

"They wanted to let you go," Sue explained. "I told them no. Then they said you could stay if you worked the pharmacy."

"They were hoping I'd quit, weren't they?" I asked.

Sue winked and patted me on the back.

"You showed them what you're made of."

Happy Feet, Happy Hands

When I took my kids to the open-captioned showing of the Warner Brothers' movie *Happy Feet*, little did I know that a bunch of penguins would stir up all of my innermost feelings about mainstreaming and the oppression of deaf children.

Oh, come on, this is a great family movie, I thought to myself. *Just put the deaf stuff on hold for once and enjoy the show, all right?*

But no matter how hard I tried, there was no escape. *Happy Feet* repeatedly drove home an important message that deaf advocates have been preaching for years.

The main character in the movie is Mumble, a penguin who can't sing worth a lick. This is significant because Mumble lives amongst a group of Emperor penguins who cherish singing above all else. In order to be accepted and find a mate, they emphasize, you've got to be able to carry a tune.

Mumble's parents are alarmed when they discover their baby can't sing. He does, however, have a knack for tap-dancing. This proves to be crucial later in the movie because—*Hey! I'm not giving away the ending. Go see for yourself.*

Nonetheless, I was struck by the reaction of Mumble's parents and the entire penguin community as a whole. Mumble winds up being referred to a music teacher in hopes that she'll be able to teach him how to sing just like everyone else.

This is where the flashbacks started hitting me hard. How could I not think back to days when I was referred to a speech therapist in hopes that I could be taught to speak just like everyone else?

And then, when Mumble eventually fails, he and his hippity-hoppity feet are sent packing. As he wanders off alone he eventually runs into a group of Adelie penguins— the Adelie Amigos. Unlike the Emperor penguins, the Adelie Amigos accept Mumble for who he is and they truly appreciate his dancing ability.

Another flashback. How could I not think back to the days when I first enrolled at Gallaudet University, where I could finally be myself and be fully accepted as the deaf man that I am?

I'm amazed at how an animated film could be so deep, even if the writers aren't aware that they just hit a home run on behalf of the deaf community. You could easily switch the penguins' singing vs. dancing conflict to the one involving speaking vs. signing for deaf children.

If you've read Gina Oliva's *Alone in the Mainstream: A Deaf Woman Remembers Public School* or Dennis Jones Jr.'s *Tarnished Halos and Crooked Fences: A Journey into the World of the Deaf and Hard of Hearing*, then you can easily see the parallel.

I can just see my 6'7" buddy Dennis Jones Jr. shaking his head at the realization that I've compared him to a penguin. Regardless, his book—and Oliva's— are a must-read if you want to see the stress deaf people endure when they're pressured to conform to mainstream ideals.

Clearly, the message the movie intended to convey was the importance of accepting people for who they are. So the next time you see people pooh-poohing deaf children's right to interact with their true peers via the language they are most comfortable with, invite them to watch *Happy Feet*. And then, after they're visibly touched by this beautiful movie, tell them you have happy *hands* and deserve to use them. If this doesn't help them get it, nothing will.

Mainstreaming vs. Deaf School Part II

In a previous article titled *Mainstreaming vs. Deaf School (Baseball Version)* I made a promise regarding my deaf son. Here are my exact words:

The next camp Darren goes to, baseball or anything else, is going to be a deaf camp. There is simply no substitute for being around your real peers.

To recap the events that led to this promise, Darren had an opportunity the year before to participate in a top-quality baseball camp. But was it top-quality interaction? With a couple hundred hearing kids? Unfortunately, no.

Since Darren has an immense love for baseball, I figured he'd make the most of the experience. And he did. He succeeded in terms of improving his baseball skills. But there was still something wrong with the picture. Literally.

When the official team picture arrived at our house a few weeks later, I was taken aback at Darren's expression. His teammates were grinning from ear to ear. Darren, on the other hand, looked like he was sitting in the waiting room at the dentist's office.

A heart-to-heart talk with Darren revealed what I'd known all along: Spending the entire day with hearing kids who don't sign isn't easy.

Advocates for inclusion will throw out the usual *but it's a hearing world* argument and insist this is for the better good. Oh, please. We're talking summer camp. We're talking about having a good time, not stressing to fit in.

So what did we do? The following summer we took a three-camp approach and boy, did we ever learn something.

The first camp we sent Darren to was Camp Overbrook: IN SIGN. It was a two-week camp for deaf and hard of hearing children sponsored by the Deaf Apostolate under the Archdiocese of Philadelphia.

The difference was remarkable. Upon arriving home from a full day at camp, Darren would excitedly talk—in detail—about what he had learned. He talked about the camp's guest speakers and performers, and he talked about new friends got to know on a much deeper level.

At last year's baseball camp, Darren would often shrug and say "fine" when asked how his day went. Maybe he'd add something like "Number nine hit a triple" (without knowing the actual name of number nine) or "I pitched two innings today." At Overbrook, Darren would come home and name names. He'd repeat a joke that David told him, or talk about how he and Michael played a practical joke on Jeff. Nothing superficial. We're talking real interaction here.

At the end of camp, Darren was part of a skit put together with the help of performers from Cleveland Signstage. I don't want to make a big deal out of this because it was just a five-minute skit, not a Broadway play. But I couldn't help notice how Darren had a leading role in the skit.

Realistically speaking, if he was the only deaf kid in high school, do you think he'd get a leading role in a school play? Not likely. I've heard so many stories of deaf kids in the mainstream who don't make the basketball team, don't run for class president, and so on. I know there are exceptions, but the majority of these *solitaires* just fade away in the background.

The next camp Darren attended was the Sertoma Fantasy Baseball Camp near Harrisburg, PA. We only attended two days out of the week-long camp, but again you could see the kids interacting on a level you just don't see in the mainstream. A pool party and an evening excursion to a Harrisburg Senators minor league game were a ton of fun. There were deaf kids, hard of hearing kids, and some kids with cochlear implants. They didn't care who was what. They just had a good time. Nice to see that. I love it when kids rise above the politics of their parents and teachers.

Finally, the camp of all camps: Camp Mark Seven in Old Forge, NY. A one-week camp way up in the boondocks. This is the one I was a bit worried about. Not just because of the distance (a good six-hour drive) or the fact it would be Darren's first overnight camp.

I actually thought this camp might be *too deaf.*

Camp Mark Seven features an all-deaf, all-ASL cast of amazing camp counselors. The kids who go there are mostly from deaf families. After interacting with hearing kids a majority of his time in school and on rec baseball teams, we felt it was time for Darren to get immersed in an all-ASL environment.

But at the same time, this was an overnight camp six hours away from home. What if it was too overwhelming? After all, Darren spent most of his early years as a hearing kid before he went deaf a few years ago. He hasn't had the opportunity to meet as many other deaf kids as we would have liked. So would Camp Mark Seven be too much of a culture shock?

Not at all. The kid had the best time of his life. Camping, canoeing, visiting a water park, storytelling, swimming, and numerous other activities. He flat-out loved his camp counselors and raved about them on the ride home. He got along great with his peers. The only thing he was disappointed in was the fact that this year's camp was just for one week, not two.

"You want to go back next year?" I asked.

"Yes! Next year it's going to be two weeks!" was the enthusiastic reply. This coming from the same kid who shrugged *"Eh, it was okay"* after an exclusive baseball camp with hearing kids a year ago.

I've said this many times before and I'll say it again now. *Never underestimate the power of interacting with your true peers.* It makes a world of difference. If you have a deaf kid and you're confronted with a school district that says otherwise, show them this article.

One other issue remains. I've asked Darren in the past if he would like to go to a deaf school. He had always said no. The reason for this is because he's known all of his current hearing classmates from way back in Pre-K, when he was still hearing himself. Even after going deaf, he still feels a life-long bond with them and that's understandable.

At the same time, it's very noticeable that his interaction with his hearing friends is at its best during recreational activities such as baseball, football, or bike-riding. During indoor parties or casual gatherings, he becomes quiet and often isn't able to keep up with the conversation. Video games might break the awkward moments of silence, but that's pretty much it.

Time to pick the kid's brains again.

"Say, Darren, would you like to go to a deaf school someday?"

Once more, he replies with the same answer:

"No. I'd miss all my friends."

Now for the stumper:

"That's true. Hey, what about Camp Mark Seven? Would you like to go again?"

Once more, his eyes light up and he gives an emphatic "Yes!"

"All right," I continued. "Now what if you could go to school with all your deaf friends at Camp Mark Seven?"

This time, it hits him. He looks at me, starts to answer, and then pauses. No words come out. The silence is deafening. It was a clear paradigm shift, a reality check.

Darren never answered my question that night. He didn't have to. Nonetheless, he gained two things he didn't have before: A frame of reference, and a fascinating journey ahead of him.

Once You Go Deaf, You've Left

When my good friends Gregg and Sheryl Spera got married, I had the honor of sitting next to Harold, one of their former oral school classmates. Many of the deaf people at the wedding communicated via sign language, but not Harold. He promptly gave me a lesson on accessibility for the oral deaf.

"The priest is too far away for me to read his lips," Harold moaned. "And the interpreter is no help because I can't sign."

He also can't monitor his voice. He didn't realize it was loud enough to draw weird looks from the hearing folks around us.

"Man," he sighed, squirming in his seat. "I don't know what the fuck is going on here!"

I cringed as several people suddenly turned around to see who had the chutzpah to cuss in church. Nonetheless, I could empathize. I know what it feels like to sit at a religious service and not understand what's going on.

Tick... tock. Tick... tock. Tick... tock.

Drip... drip... drip.

Yawn.

51

Yes, it's that bad.

Sure, Harold could speak clearly. But he was still deaf. He had trouble following what others said no matter how eloquent he was. Meanwhile, my wife and I thoroughly enjoyed an ASL-inclusive wedding.

The reception had an interesting mix of people. You could tell that many of the former oral school students had gone their own separate ways. Some of them were still oral and didn't use any form of sign language. Others spoke with their voices, but accompanied their speech with signed English (this is known as sim-com, or simultaneous communication).

Another group of deaf people signed without using their voices, but their signing was a mix of signed English and Pidgin Signed English (PSE). Finally, there was a group of deaf people who signed ASL. This included Gregg and Sheryl, who count themselves amongst a growing group of former oralists who now sign fluently.

It didn't really matter to the reunited oral school students. They hugged, mingled, got along great. This was no time for deaf education politics. Regardless of whether you spoke with your voice, signed haltingly, or blew everyone away with your ASL (Gregg and Sheryl did just that—they performed an ASL song that rocked the reception hall), you were welcome regardless of your communication preference.

At the same time, I noticed a pattern amongst the signing deaf people. It reminded me of something I wrote in a grad school term paper:

Once you go deaf, you've left.

(Yes, I actually said that in a term paper. Psychosocial Aspects of Deafness, 1993.)

It's not unusual for oralists to eventually discover the joys of sign language. When they do, they embark on a journey where they pick up more ASL and become involved in the deaf community.

This is understandable. It's the entire premise of my book Deaf Again, *where an exciting Deaf world opened up once I accepted my Deaf identity.*

When I discussed this with a colleague, we came up with a fascinating question. Sure, we've seen plenty of oralists cross over to the ASL side of the continuum; but how often do we see deaf people moving in the opposite direction? We don't. You never see a signing deaf person get up and say, "Know what? Oralism is cool. I think I'm going to stop signing and just use my voice from now on."

Several years before, I had another interesting exchange with a colleague. It was with school psychologist Michelle Corallo, who identifies herself as hard of hearing.

As I passed Michelle's office one day, I noticed her speaking into a phone. I stopped in my tracks and watched her seamlessly wrap up her voice conversation. This was long before we had videophones and video relay services; back then, I had to use a clunky TDD and a ridiculously slow TDD relay service when calling hearing people on the phone. So yes, at that time it was my opinion that Michelle had the upper hand communication-wise.

"Wow, you can speak on the phone?" I asked. "Lucky you!"

Michelle looked at me as if I were crazy.

"Are you kidding?" she shot back. "I'm exhausted."

And Michelle is right. It takes a lot of work to function as a hearing person when you aren't hearing. Which is why most deaf and hard of hearing people instinctively gravitate towards their true peers once given the opportunity. So why would anyone want to deny them this opportunity?

But wait! What about children with cochlear implants? They need to be assimilated into the hearing world as much as possible to further enhance their speaking and listening skills.

Not so fast. I don't care if you wear a hearing aid or a cochlear implant. I don't care if you're prelingually deaf, postlingually deaf, or deaf by virtue of alien abduction experiment gone bad. If you have any degree of deafness— be it mild, moderate or profound—you probably would like to meet other people who are just like you. And that goes just the same for kids with cochlear implants.

Think I'm wrong? Then go visit Gallaudet University or the National Technical Institute for the Deaf (NTID). Look at how many students have cochlear implants. There are a lot of them. The numbers have grown significantly over the years and will continue to grow. And we will continue to see many of these implanted students choosing to attend college with other deaf students in a more communicatively accessible environment. What does this indicate?

Many of these students with cochlear implants will say that regardless of their level of success—and that level of success widely varies amongst them—they still have a core group of deaf and hard of hearing friends with whom they can relax and be themselves. Again, why would anyone want to deny them this opportunity?

Too much emphasis on the ears and the mouth instead of the whole person, that's why.

I'd like to wrap this up with another eye-opening social experience involving my son Darren. At age ten he successfully tried out for the Montgomery Wolverines, a 10u travel team. Although there were times when he misunderstood the coaches and wasn't able to keep up with group conversations, for the most part he enjoyed himself. He loves baseball so much that he's willing to tolerate the occasional awkward silence. He was also familiar with most of the players, as he had previously played with many of them in his rec baseball league. With all of this in mind, I wasn't too concerned about him feeling left out. Besides, practice and games moved at a fast pace and rarely went beyond two hours. All was good and the kid had a great time.

By the time Darren was twelve, the Wolverines decided to participate in a week-long national tournament in Cooperstown, New York. This time, I had some concerns.

Playing on the field for two hours is fine. Staying overnight in the dorm as the only deaf player in the entire camp? Not so good. Still, this tournament was an opportunity we could not turn down.

Our solution? Darren was permitted to bring his cell phone and text me as much as he wanted. If the dorm experience were to become excruciatingly boring, I'd come pick him up and let him stay with me in the apartment I'd rented three miles away.

Darren had a wonderful time. He played on the immaculately-kept fields at Cooperstown Dreams Park (the closest most kids ever get to knowing what it feels like to play in the pros). He batted .400. He had a memorable visit to the Cooperstown Hall of Fame. He wrote a powerful letter explaining why deaf baseball player William Ellsworth "Dummy" Hoy deserves to be in the Hall of Fame. He had an awe-inspiring meeting with Brad Horn, Senior Director of Communications and Education at the Hall of Fame, when he turned in the aforementioned letter. All in all, it was a remarkable experience we'll never forget.

And yet...

The kid texted me incessantly.

At breakfast, lunch, dinner, and during evening social time, my cell phone wouldn't stop buzzing. I think I talked to Darren via text messages that week more than I spoke to him in person all year. Needless to say, the cell phone communication filled in admirably whenever Darren felt lost in the crowd. On top of that, a couple of times I took him out of camp for dinner. It all worked out beautifully.

And then...

The following week Darren went to Camp Mark Seven. An all-deaf camp in Old Forge, New York. Deaf staff. Deaf campers. Everyone signing. Nonetheless, seeing how much Darren appreciated having his cell phone with him in Cooperstown, I decided to let him keep the phone with him at Camp Mark Seven as well.

"Have fun, dude." I patted him on the back as I dropped him off. "Text me soon and let me know how you're doing."

The kid didn't text me for four days.

Darren was too busy having fun around the clock with his deaf peers the way he was supposed to. The cell phone silence spoke volumes.

I can't emphasize this enough. We all need that stress-free environment where we can be ourselves amongst our true peers. Just ask Michelle. And be sure to duck when she throws the phone at you.

Part II
Understanding the Madness

Diagnostic Crisis

During a first grade music class—back in the days when I thought I had perfectly normal hearing—I belted the following tune:

My gal rode the boat outdoors with Al and Louie, yeah!

The teacher actually froze at the piano.

"Um, Mark..." she inquired. "Could you repeat what you just said?"

I was only too happy to oblige.

My gal road the boat outdoors with Al and Louie, yeah!

Our music teacher was a gentle, elderly woman well into her sixties. I think I drove her into retirement. But before she left, she took the time to correct the lyrics I'd butchered to pieces.

"Mark... the actual words are *Michael row the boat ashore, hallelujah.*"

A new Deaf world had opened. After a series of similar misunderstandings, soon I found myself in my grandfather's apartment. A phone call from my teacher had him greatly concerned. I was only five years old at the time but I could clearly tell that something was wrong.

"Can you understand what I'm saying?" My grandfather asked.

"Yeah, sure," I replied.

"Okay, now let's try it this way." My grandfather covered his mouth with his hand and spoke again.

"Howbout rhynow? Cnu erwt imsyng? Mrk, cnu unrand me?"

"What? Uh, yes?"

My grandfather's eyes widened in horror. He realized that what my teachers had said was true. This set off a chain of events where I would wind up visiting many a doctor, audiologist, and speech/language pathologist.

And just like that, my Deaf world had slammed shut.

For many parents of deaf children, such a discovery can be very traumatic. All sense of normalcy flies out the window. They see a handicap, a disability, a medical problem. It hurts. Understandably, this turn of events triggers a grieving process. Shock, denial, anger, depression, the whole works.

During a Psychosocial Aspects of Deafness course in grad school, I learned that this is a common reaction that's often referred to as the *diagnostic crisis*. As far as the grieving process goes, what makes it even more complicated is the fact that the parents are not grieving a dead person.

They're grieving for someone who is very much alive, and in the process can greatly influence this person.

A side note for parents: If you're a parent of a deaf child and this is the first time you've read anything in depth about ASL and Deaf culture, it is my sincere hope that you'll find this information both entertaining and useful.

But in the never-ending search for answers, I kindly request that you remember to do one very important thing: Please include deaf people when you ask any questions about what it means to be deaf.

Can you imagine me going on Oprah *and telling the world what it means to be a woman? I could probably give a scientific, biological account of female anatomy, pregnancy, menopause, and whatnot.*

But I would never be able to tell you what it means, or what it feels like, to be a woman. Only an actual woman could do that.

Likewise, if you truly want to understand the essence of what it means to be deaf, you have to ask a deaf person. And it would be best to ask several deaf people because we all have our own varying beliefs and experiences. But they are very real beliefs and experiences, and you stand to benefit from that information as much as (if not more than) anything a medical professional might tell you.

Introjection

Before we can go into the importance of a healthy deaf identity, we need to examine a fascinating phenomenon known as the *introject*. Dolly Schulman, the Director of the Modern Gestalt Institute in Wayne, Pennsylvania, introduced me to the concept of introjection during her year-long course in Gestalt Theory & Practice.

Introjection is basically known as a resistance where we (paraphrasing Erving & Miriam Polster in *Gestalt Therapy Integrated: Contours of Theory & Practice*) "incorporate what the environment provides," "swallow whole impressions of the world," and "give up a sense of free choice in life."

Introjects, then, are a powerful influence that literally program our minds and shape our behavior. Let's take a look at a few examples. Below are some apparently harmless quotes that kids are exposed to on a daily basis:

Finish your plate.

If you don't stop making goofy faces, your face will freeze like that.

Big boys don't cry.

You should...

As I said, apparently harmless. But if you take a closer look, words like these have more power than we ever could have imagined. For example, let's break down *big boys don't cry.*

I guarantee you that at any movie theater in the country, if you observe a man and a woman going to a movie together, you'll find an interesting contrast in behavior.

If the movie has a strong emotional impact—be it a heart-tugging happy ending or a tear-jerking tragedy—you can bet that the woman has no qualms about sniffling and sobbing in full view of everyone.

The guy, on the other hand, is more fun to watch. He'll gulp. His lips will quiver. He'll pretend he's got something stuck in his eye. If you ask him if he's okay, he'll swear nothing's wrong. He'll emit a fake yawn, stretch out his arms, and discreetly brush away a tear. If you observe this behavior long enough you'd think this guy was ready for a straitjacket.

It wasn't the movie that wigged him out. You have to go back in time to locate the source of his strange behavior. So, imagine this man several years ago when he was a little kid; he's playing football in the backyard with some family and friends when all of a sudden, he slips and scrapes his knee. Naturally, he starts crying. And then someone says the magic words: *Oh, come on, suck it up! Big boys don't cry, you big baby.*

That's all it takes. This boy has now been programmed by an introject. He absorbs and internalizes this message. It becomes his reality. And then, twenty years later, you can find him in the movie theater having a spastic fit.

Introjects don't have to be verbal. Kids watch their parents' behavior and internalize just about anything. The age-old curse "*I hope someday you wind up having kids just like you!*" definitely works. Like it or not, most of us emulate our parents in ways that are quite uncanny. Without even realizing it, many kids literally walk, talk, and have certain idiosyncrasies exactly like their parents.

And now we're ready to bring this discussion back to deaf identity. With the previous examples in mind, what do the following introjects tell you?

Sit up front.

Wear your hearing aids.

Read my lips.

Hearing-impaired.

Yes, when we utter the above words to deaf children all over the world, we're instilling in them a model of deficit thinking. We're telling these kids that deafness is bad, that they're "impaired," that they need to be fixed. We're telling them that they need to look, think, and act like hearing people. And, with hearing aids and speech therapy galore, we're giving the impression that it's entirely the deaf child's responsibility to assimilate.

These introjects can weigh down a deaf person for a lifetime. It's a formidable obstacle to overcome.

Removing the Mask

I t never ceases to amaze me how, in their efforts to appease the predominantly hearing environment around them, deaf children will often go to great lengths to trick people into thinking they can understand everyone just fine.

Nothing illustrates this point clearer than what happened in the summer of 1999. As a guest speaker at the Governor Baxter School for the Deaf's Family Learning Vacation, I was asked to run a group session with deaf and hard of hearing children. Most of these kids were between the ages of ten and thirteen. After getting to know them for a few minutes I decided to toss them the following question:

What do you do at family events where you're the only deaf or hard of hearing person and no one knows sign language?

One of the answers floored me. There was this one kid, about twelve years old, who said:

"I say hello... and then run!"

I asked him what he meant by "run." He explained that he would approach his relatives on a one-by-one basis, engage in some superficial conversation, and then make a hasty retreat before it evolved beyond "How are you,"

"How's the family," and "How's school." Unbeknownst to virtually everyone, this kid was manipulating each and every conversation.

He was an expert at lipreading superficial conversation because he knew what to look for. But he also knew that if anyone changed the subject he would have been like a deer frozen in the headlights. So he took control, mastered the art of how-do-ya-do, and moved on as quickly as possible.

This kid definitely has a future in politics. He may not understand what people are saying, but he sure knows how to work a room.

"Isn't that exhausting?" I asked.

"Yeah," he admitted, with several of the other kids nodding affirmatively. "Sometimes I sneak out and go to my room to play Nintendo for a while."

This was one of the best group discussions I'd ever seen. It was not just the young boy's confession that struck me hard—it was also the knowing looks on the other kids' faces. This twelve-year-old kid had validated the experiences and frustrations of everyone else in the room that day.

It seems crazy, but it's what we do. The introjects of our previous lesson—*sit up front, wear your hearing aids, read my lips,* et cetera—ingrain it into the deaf or hard of hearing child's mind that the responsibility for effective communication rests entirely on his or her tiny shoulders. What a load to carry! And we react in strange ways indeed, as our twelve-year-old friend confessed.

There's a long-term consequence for this kind of lifestyle. When we strain to understand what people are saying—no matter if we eventually do understand or just smile and nod—there's a very real physical reaction. It comes back to bite us further down the road.

When we don't understand what people are saying, that's stress. When we put in the effort to try harder, that's more stress. If we succeed, it only opens the door to more conversation and the cycle repeats itself. When we fail, we feel bad and perhaps blame ourselves. After all, we've assumed all the responsibility for communicating with the hearing world.

Dr. Samuel Trychin—who, incidentally, also happens to be hard of hearing—has documented that the stress of *sit up front, wear your hearing aids, read my lips*, et cetera, can lead to very real physical symptoms later in life. In his fascinating research (check out his web page at http://trychin.com/) Dr. Trychin lists muscle tension, back pain, fatigue, high blood pressure, irritability, anxiety, stomach problems, and other symptoms as a very real consequence to the *sit-up-front-read-my-lips* lifestyle.

I can personally vouch that this is true. After years of being The Only Deaf Guy, a back injury sent me to a physical therapist. She told me that never before had she encountered someone whose muscles were so tightly wound. My back was like a high-tension rubber band that was ready to snap.

And so we've identified a very real problem that manifests not just in mental strain but physical strain as well. The overcome this, it takes tremendous self-awareness and a paradigm shift.

I've mentioned many times that deaf and hard of children are remarkably adept at the infamous Art of Nodding. As a self-described walking bobblehead doll, I know a thing or two about nodding. In fact, that's what I did all the way from kindergarten up to the ninth grade.

There was this routine I followed everyday: *Sit up front, wear your hearing aids, read lips, and look like you were on top of things even if you were totally clueless.* At the end of each class I'd discreetly ask a classmate for that day's homework. I often had to do extra reading to catch up on missed material so that I could adequately finish my assignments.

Thanks to this routine I was barely able to be a "C" student. That's "C" as in *Cunning, Clever, Crafty, Compensating,* and *Convincing.* "C" also stands for *Chameleon,* which is exactly what I tried to be in my efforts to blend in amongst hearing people.

Fortunately, my teachers were able to see through the charade. They knew I was in survival mode and that something had to change if I were to succeed during the latter years of high school. They decided the best course of action would be to hire an ASL interpreter. (Considering this was in the early '80s, long before the Americans with Disabilities Act went into effect, my high school—Germantown Friends School—deserves a ton of respect for being way ahead of the times.)

Unfortunately, I was too much a prisoner of my own introjects to be able to see where my teachers were going with this. I vehemently protested against the concept of some stranger walking into class and following me around like a parole officer. I wound up having to meet with a child psychologist before finally agreeing to give ASL interpreting a shot.

Remember, introjects are incredibly powerful. And a solitary deaf student in an all-hearing high school is *not* going to thump his chest and hand out *Deaf Pride* paraphernalia. ASL was nothing to be proud of. I was downright embarrassed.

In fact, look at it this way: How does the typical teenager react when he wakes up with a zit? It's something along the lines of *Oh my god, my life is over! I'm gonna diiie! Mom, can I stay home? Let me pop this thing. Oh crap, look at it now! If you make me go to school like this I'm going to wear a bag over my head. Is there a sandblaster that can fix my face?*

Yes, teenagers are incredibly self-conscious. So imagine telling a deaf teenager in an all-hearing school that he needs to wear a hearing aid. A hearing aid weighs only a few ounces but believe me, it can feel like fifty pounds. Now imagine telling this kid who wants nothing more than to blend in with all the hearing folks that he's going to have his own personal translator following him all over the place. Not good.

That's exactly how I felt. But in relatively short time, I was won over by my interpreter. You see, an ASL interpreter in high school doesn't seem like a good idea until one compares the following formulas:

SUF + WYHA / RL + B = 25% Access

(Sit Up Front + Wear Your Hearing Aids / Read Lips and Bluff)

1CDG + ASLint = 100% Access

(One Clueless Deaf Guy + ASL interpreter)

The first time my interpreter unleashed those flying hands, my eyes widened in absolute amazement. I simply could not believe the amount of information that was coming in. I was flabbergasted at how much I could understand. I was even more incredulous—mad at myself, even—over how much information I'd missed prior to getting an interpreter.

Why hadn't anyone told me about this before? Like, say, in first grade?

Both the amount of information and the ease of how I was able to absorb it completely changed the way I looked at school. For once, it was an enjoyable learning experience. Here are four reasons why this was so:

1. *The "Aaaaaaaah" factor.* Face it, there's simply no comparison. Which would you rather do: Crane your neck and try to follow a teacher's lips as she paces the classroom, and only be able to understand twenty-five to thirty-five percent of what she's saying? Or, just kick back and effortlessly understand everything an interpreter signs in ASL? For me, an interpreter was so relaxing. No more straining, struggling, wondering, or filling in the blanks. In ASL, all of the information was effortlessly absorbed.

2. *One hundred percent accessibility.* Okay, one hundred percent might be a stretch. *Nothing* is understood perfectly. There are misunderstandings, moments of attention deficit, and occasionally things get lost in translation. But again, compared to lipreading, ASL is light years ahead in terms of ability to absorb educational content. Like I said, there simply is no comparison.

3. *No more bugging classmates for missed material.* This is a benefit for both student and teacher. The student doesn't have to stress over finding someone who can fill in the blanks regarding missed assignments. The teacher can take satisfaction in knowing that the *Duh, I didn't know there was a homework assignment* excuse doesn't fly anymore.

4. *Significantly enhanced ability to learn from classmates.* One of the biggest surprises the first day I got an ASL interpreter was seeing—for the first time—the amount of input the other students had. Previously, I'd tuned them out because it was hard enough just trying to read the teacher's lips.

70

(Everyone else? Feh. Not worth the effort.) But with the interpreter, *bam!* I suddenly realized that other students had a lot to offer in terms of classroom discussion. That's when it hit me that in addition to learning from the teacher, students are supposed to learn from each other.

In addition to the above four benefits, a fifth one gradually appears. When ASL is incorporated into the classroom—and when a deaf student sees that not only do the teachers approve of it but it's also accepted by other students—there's a paradigm shift that works its way into the mix.

Remember all of those old introjects?

Sit up front. Wear your hearing aid. Read my lips. It's your responsibility to assimilate into the mainstream.

Now we have a different message making itself clear:

Hey, ASL is accepted. It's okay to be different. Yes, that's it: I'm not disabled, I'm just different.

We are now moving away from the *deficit model* and moving towards the *difference model.*

Met Deaf, Wow!

In the PBS documentary *Through Deaf Eyes* there's an interview segment with Gina Oliva, the author of *Alone in the Mainstream: A Deaf Woman Remembers Public School.*

Gina hit the nail on the head for thousands of deaf people everywhere when she shared her solitary mainstream experience. Having been mainstreamed for several years, Gina eventually attended Gallaudet University. It was at the world's only university for the deaf where she finally met other people who were *exactly like her.*

In the aforementioned documentary, Gina came up with the ASL phrase *Met Deaf, Wow!* to describe the shock, the joy, and the awe that comes with meeting your true peers after years of isolation in the mainstream.

I totally understand. The same thing happened to me when I enrolled at Gallaudet in 1989. I will never forget my immersion into an all-deaf environment. It was pure nirvana.

Gallaudet University is the first place where I found one hundred percent communication accessibility around the clock. Not only was it real-time accessibility (communicating directly with people as opposed to a three-second delay with an interpreter) but it went way beyond regular school hours.

In high school, I had an ASL interpreter from 8:00 a.m. to 3:00 p.m. That was it. After the last class was over I went back into my usual fog. But at Gallaudet, there was no end to communication access. Easily understandable ASL conversations took place in the classroom, amongst friends walking in the hallways, in the cafeteria, at sports events, in the dorm, and so on. Communication never stopped. Not once was I ever left out of a conversation no matter where I was.

From this experience comes the *I didn't know what I was missing* epiphany. It happens like this:

Many deaf students, myself included, often pat ourselves on the back for making it in the mainstream. On top of that you also have parents, teachers, support staff, and medical professionals heaping praise on a mainstream student for being "brave" and "fitting in just like any other normal student." Those of us with deaf voices and accents are often told we're doing wonderful in speech therapy—further misleading us into thinking we've mastered The Art of Looking and Talking Just Like a Normal Hearing Person. And, with no frame of reference, we suck it all in. We fall for it hook, line, and sinker. We truly believe we've got it made.

But after the inevitable *Met Deaf, Wow!* experience, we often look back on those days with a more realistic view. Armed with a frame of reference, many of us come to understand that we'd only been faking it—that in retrospect, there was clearly so much we missed out on in the mainstream. If only we'd known!

A classic example is my experience playing baseball on both hearing and deaf teams. During my childhood days in the mainstream I truly had a fantastic time playing baseball on Little League, Pony League, High School and Summer Rec League teams.

Actually, I had a great time *on the field*. Then I'd contentedly stare out the window while numerous teammates engaged in conversation on the bus ride back to school or the rec center. *Hey, I contributed to the team!* That was good enough for me. Many coaches marveled at how this brave deaf kid played "just as well as any normal hearing kid." I fit in! Or did I?

Years later, on the Gallaudet University baseball team, I not only played the game but also took part in strategic dialogue on the field and in the dugout. After each road game, I found myself fully absorbed in conversation and jokes with my teammates on the bus ride back to campus. When we stopped somewhere for dinner, there would be even more conversation and jokes, and again I was able to enjoy total access and participation. Only after experiencing this was I able to reminisce about the numerous seasons I'd played for hearing teams and suddenly realize that back then, *I didn't know what I was missing.*

Here's some food for thought: These experiences at Gallaudet should be the *norm* for deaf and hard of hearing kids all the way through K-12. But, thanks to PL 94-142, which evolved into the Individuals with Disabilities Education Act (IDEA), countless deaf kids are denied such an opportunity.

As for me, I didn't enroll at Gallaudet until I was twenty-three years old. *Twenty-three!* Do you want the next generation of deaf kids to wait that long before they can say *Met Deaf, Wow?*

Gallaudet offered a long overdue, highly enjoyable learning experience. And when you consider the communication accessibility in the classroom, dorms, cafeteria, sports events, theater events, and anything

74

else all over campus, we have a new series of introjects replacing the old. Gone were:

Sit up front.
Wear your hearing aids.
Read my lips.
Hearing-impaired.

In their place were:

We're all the same here.
No special treatment. You're fine.
Yes you can. In fact, you can do better.
Deaf people can do anything except hear.
Look at all these deaf role models. If they can do it,
you can too.

I can't say enough about deaf role models. When you meet deaf doctors, lawyers, engineers, teachers, entrepreneurs, artists, entertainers, et cetera—of which there are plenty at Gallaudet and the surrounding Metro Washington region—you can't help but be inspired. A self-imposed glass ceiling held up by old introjects suddenly shatters. The new introjects clearly indicate the sky's the limit.

Signing With The Fockers

I n the movie *Meet the Fockers*, Robert DeNiro plays an obsessed grandfather hell-bent on teaching ASL to his infant grandson. He's fully aware of the cognitive and linguistic benefits that come with early exposure to ASL. He understands that babies are able to build a solid language base in ASL long before their vocal cords develop. It's a logical head start.

What's illogical, then, is that in spite of the baby sign language craze that followed after the movie—in spite of research dating back to the '80s that validate its effectiveness—there are still plenty of people out there who deny *deaf* babies the opportunity to learn sign language.

This piqued my interest to the point where I decided to take a closer look at how I communicate at home. With my two older sons (born in 1999 and 2001), my wife and I have always used ASL and English. It's truly a bilingual household. But we didn't give it much thought because hey, we're deaf. It's only natural that we sign at home.

By the time my daughter Lacey was born in June of 2005, I'd seen enough controversy out there to realize it was time to do some personal research. I wanted specific numbers and data to back up my overwhelmingly positive experience.

76

Armed with a copy of *The Baby Book: Everything You Need to Know About Your Baby—From Birth to Age Two* (by William Sears, M.D. and Martha Sears, R.N.), I learned that the following is considered normal language development for (non-signing) babies between nine and twelve months of age:

- Can make two-syllable sounds such as "ma-ma" or "da-da"

- Associates sounds with the right person

- Understands "no"

- Can imitate sounds

- Understands gestures (such as waving bye-bye)

Now have a frame of reference for a signing baby. Here's what Lacey had at a very early age:

- An extended vocabulary including words and names such as *Mommy, Daddy, Darren, Brandon, Grandmom, funny, water, baby, The Wiggles, finished, all gone, yes, no, bye-bye, ball, dog, cat, eat, sleep, potty, bath, Elmo, Cookie Monster, Big Bird,* and more.

- Ability to communicate in multiple-word sentences such as *"Where's the kitty cat? "Where's the ball?" "Found it!" "Daddy's funny" "Lacey got a boo-boo" "Diaper stinks, whew!"* and more.

What makes this eye-opening is the fact that Lacey was signing all of those words and sentences by the tender age of *eleven months.* According to *The Baby Book*, it's usually around eighteen to twenty-four months when a hearing, non-signing baby approaches this level of communication

77

(and speaking in sentences is actually more common between twenty-four and thirty-six months).

Lacey isn't alone. There are other signing babies, both deaf and hearing, who are doing the same thing. I have several deaf friends raising babies of their own and it's fascinating to watch them all signing at remarkably early ages.

Unfortunately, when a baby is identified as deaf these days, the odds are more likely that he or she will be nudged towards a path that avoids sign language as much as possible.

Look, I'm not an absolutist; if a deaf or hard of hearing child prefers auditory-verbal methods and would much rather use speech and technology to get by in this world, I'm fine with it. I'm just saying that at the earliest stages of life, a baby—any baby—has the ability to communicate with its hands long before his or her vocal cords develop.

This is an opportunity to stimulate the brain with language at a remarkably early age.

The benefits are irrefutable. A mind wired for language, a higher IQ, an expanded vocabulary, fewer temper tantrums, more bonding with parents... who wouldn't want this?

There are just so many "oral failures" who slip through the cracks and go through their lives with unrecoverable language delays. Signing in infancy is a bona fide insurance policy that can prevent this. If a baby starts out with ASL and then later jettisons it because he or she is more comfortable with an auditory-verbal approach, I don't have a problem with that. If the auditory-verbal approach works for a particular child, fine. If not, then the kid still has a solid language base that was built much earlier thanks to ASL.

And there are plenty of deaf children for whom speech is *not* a good option. For these kids, a visual method of instruction is much more efficient. They absolutely fly when they have the opportunity to learn in ASL.

Think about it: Would you rather spend hours trying to get a kid to correctly pronounce "George Washington," or would you rather quickly explain in ASL just what exactly it was that this Mr. Washington did that was so important? Why pound a square peg into a round hole?

Also, keep in mind that it doesn't have to be either/or. You'd be surprised at how many deaf people can both speak and sign. Contrary to popular myth, one communication method does not cause the other to suffer. Plenty of deaf kids have the ability to code switch between the two languages. (Yes, English and ASL are two separate languages. Don't let anyone tell you different.) Many kids can easily become fluent in several different languages—in fact, it's much easier for children than adults—so there's nothing wrong with a child learning Spanish, French, Russian, German...and ASL.

Last but not least, back to the ever-expanding baby sign language craze: it's gone beyond babies. According to the Modern Language Association of America, there was a 432 percent increase in enrollment in higher education ASL classes between the years of 1998 and 2002. So in addition to hearing babies, we now have hearing college students learning ASL en masse. (Incidentally, several high schools are now hopping on the bandwagon.)

This is an exciting development and it gives us hope for the future. It gives us hope that the next generation of deaf children will be more likely to encounter people in the world at large who have a better understanding of ASL and Deaf culture.

It's a beautiful thing. If you can't take my word for it, ask Robert DeNiro.

Breakthrough

Although I and countless other deaf advocates do our best to shed more light on the deaf experience, we still encounter plenty of resistance in the mainstream world. It's understandable, really.

Going back to the diagnostic crisis mentioned earlier in this book, most parents go through a mourning process when they first discover their child is deaf. They're mourning the loss of their hearing child. Never mind that the child is still very much alive and has a ton of potential. The possibility of a deaf child thriving in today's cold cruel world often doesn't look good to most parents.

The first line of support for these parents is often hospital staff or other professionals in the medical field. Of course these people are going to do their best to fix the physical aspect of the problem—that's their job. Hearing aids, speech therapy, cochlear implants, etc., will be the first (and probably only) options a parent of a deaf child encounters.

From there, the ideal of *fitting in* with the hearing world gains momentum. The concept that the presence or absence of sound has little to do with a person's overall happiness simply doesn't register with the world at large. So the battle to get deaf kids to *fit in* rages on.

What the world at large doesn't realize, however, is that such a battle can actually seem quite absurd—unethical, even—if viewed in a different light. For example:

- If you took one kid of a particular race or ethnic group and placed him in a school where all of the other kids were of a different race or ethnicity, you can bet this one minority kid would feel uncomfortable. You can also bet his parents wouldn't be too happy and that they'd take immediate action to remedy the situation. Put one girl in an all-boys school or a boy in an all-girls school and you'll get the same result. However, it's deemed perfectly acceptable to take one deaf kid and place him in a school where everyone else is hearing.

- If you pulled aside children of any racial or ethnic minority and told them they needed to work on acting more white, they and their families would understandably be insulted. However, it's perfectly acceptable to take a deaf kid and spend countless hours teaching him how to look and talk like a hearing person.

- It's perfectly acceptable for hearing babies, hearing high school students, and hearing college students to learn ASL. Deaf babies and deaf children, on the other hand, are often denied this opportunity.

- Deaf peers and role models are undeniably powerful, positive influences. But to this very day, I still meet hearing parents of deaf children who have been told to avoid deaf people and sign language at all costs.

- If a teacher at any school went on a leave of absence and his or her replacement spoke no English, you can bet there'd be a furor and parents would have this substitute teacher removed. But when a teacher in a deaf school is replaced by someone with little or no signing skill, most people don't make an issue out of it.

As you can see, the primary focus for most deaf children in today's world is to get them to *fit in*—sometimes at the expense of their human rights. The problem with this is that a lot of us forget it's more important to find a place where we *belong*. Let me repeat this comparison for emphasis:

Fitting in takes effort. It's exhausting and you can argue that it's not really genuine because to one degree or the other, it involves trying to win other people's approval.

Belonging is a far more rewarding phenomenon where you can kick back, be yourself, and know you are accepted. This is far more authentic and often happens in the presence of one's true peers.

Too many deaf and hard of hearing kids are forced to fit in. They're alone and on their own in the mainstream. Once again I refer you to Gina Oliva's captivating book, *Alone in the Mainstream: A Deaf Woman Remembers Public School* for numerous interviews, quotes, examples, and research that reveal the unfortunate *solitaire* experience that is the norm for many mainstreamed students all over the country.

I also refer you to an anthology titled *On the Fence: The Hidden World of the Hard of Hearing* where several writers of all ages confessed to similar frustrating experiences. I can assure you with utmost confidence that my stories and anecdotes are not just one person's experience. There are thousands, if not millions, who are in the same boat. It's time to wake up.

I woke up. Connecting with deaf peers and role models led to several *a-ha!* insights where I finally understood the behaviors of my past.

I finally understood why I continued to participate in grade school and junior high school choir classes (lip-synching, of course) after that *My Gal Road the Boat Outdoors* fiasco in first grade. I finally understood why I had "nodded" with so many hearing family, friends, and teachers. I finally understood why I tolerated the Dinner Table Syndrome for so many years. I finally understood why I worked hard to live the life that other people wanted me to live. And most important of all, I understood that it was my deaf peers and role models who allowed me to throw away the mask. You'll never catch me being inauthentic again.

In the Gestalt Theory & Practice course I took under the tutelage of Dolly Schulman, there was a lot of emphasis on authentic living. Learning about introjects was icing on the cake. The recommended intervention for introjection is as follows:

Establish within the individual a sense of choices.

You'd be amazed at the impact this remarkably simple guideline could have on deaf children all over the world. It's still a sad truth that for many deaf kids, a communication method that works isn't offered until after they've already failed at a sequential list of preferred options as recommended by a medical specialist or a school district.

But could you imagine how much better it would be if *all* options were fairly presented at the very beginning? Wouldn't it be great if parents could *immediately* select the option(s) that best meet the specific needs of their children, or if they had a Plan B to fall back on right away if Plan A didn't work out? Just imagine how different things would be if people were a bit more open-minded.

Yes, it's that simple. And this brings us to another powerful quote, one of my favorites from e.e. cummings:

The hardest fight a man has to fight is to live in a world where every single day someone is trying to make you someone you do not want to be.

Part III
More Madness

Eye Candy

During 1984 Senior Week in Wildwood, New Jersey, my girlfriend Karen roomed with some girls from her graduating class. Senior Week was, and still is, a rite of passage where high school students flock to the Jersey Shore the week after graduation. What goes on during Senior Week is not condoned by the schools of the graduating students. There are no chaperones and all hell typically breaks loose. So of course, I gladly showed up when invited to join the fun.

Karen invited me to her motel at 6:00 p.m. the first night. I was under the impression that there was going to be a party at her place. I misunderstood. The party was actually an hour later at another motel a few blocks away. Karen had asked me over a little earlier to keep her company while her roommates took forever to get dolled up.

Yes, I was the only deaf person there. Karen could communicate pretty well via ASL and she often doubled as an interpreter in countless social situations.

Bless her for going out of her way to include me in her social circle the way that she did. But for me to have to be dependent on her like that, you could see quite clearly that this relationship was doomed.

As I sat down next to Karen, one of her roommates turned the radio on and cheesy '80s music blared from the speakers. Back then, I could still hear well enough to learn some of the songs and sign along with them. Michael Jackson's *Billie Jean* was one of the songs that I could easily follow. As the unmistakable opening drum beat began, Karen and I were on our feet. We performed our ASL version of the song and her roommates were impressed. They started grooving to the beat and—

HEY! They're all prancing around in their underwear!

That's right. It was a massive display of eye candy. As Karen's roommates showered, changed, and poofed up their hair, they did so in wanton disregard of the fact that there was a guy in their presence. The music must have sent them over the edge.

Thank you, Michael Jackson!

It took every ounce of willpower to look nonchalant. One *hubba hubba* out of me and Karen probably would have thrown me out. But I was perplexed. What were these ladies doing? Why were they putting on a Vegas striptease for the hapless deaf guy?

One of them walked right past me wearing nothing more than a bra and panties. Another girl stepped out of the shower, wrapped a towel around her curvaceous body, and sat next to me as she waited for her turn to blow-dry her hair in front of the mirror.

Oh, there's more. Yet another roommate kept dressing and undressing in plain view as she couldn't make up her mind what she wanted to wear. To make matters worse (or better, from my point of view), she became equally indecisive about her underwear.

"This bra makes my boobs look saggy," she whined. "Maybe I should wear the purple one." She picked up the other bra and took a good look at it.

"Yeah," she nodded approvingly. "This one." She reached around her back and started to unhinge her bra. My heart rate shot through the stratosphere.

The only logical explanation for this is that God was paying me back for all of the crap I'd put up with in the mainstream.

Just as the bra was about to fall to the ground and reveal the heavenly mounds of forbidden fruit, there was a knock on the door.

Aw, dammit!

It was Ms. Mounds' boyfriend. All of a sudden the room erupted into total chaos.

"Oh my god! It's Mike!"

"Shit! Don't open the door!"

"I'm not ready! I'm not ready!"

"Who took my bra?"

"I don't have any makeup on!"

It was like cockroaches scurrying under the fridge after someone turned the light on. In thirty frenzied seconds, every girl in the room was fully clothed.

Damn.

As Mike walked in the door, I looked over at Karen. I couldn't make sense out of what just happened.

"I don't get it," I said. "Your friends walk around half-naked in front of me and it's okay. Then Mike shows up and they go 'Eeeeeeeek!' How come it's okay for me but not for him?"

"Oh, it's different," Karen laughed. "They're comfortable around you."

"How is it different?" I asked. "They know Mike more than they know me."

"Yeah, but… you're not really… you're no—I can't really explain it. It's fine. They love you."

Karen was being nice. She stopped herself short of saying the truth.

89

You're nothing to them.

That's right. I was the harmless wallflower. Sitting in the corner, fake smile, a deaf pet rock.

Later at the party, Karen occasionally interpreted what other people said, but it was like looking in from the outside. Even with the best interpreters it's still like everything is on three-second delay. You're not really in the moment. You're not relevant.

Fuck this, I muttered to myself. *I don't think I belong here.*

It would take another good five years until I found a place where I belonged.

The Fourth Hole

"**M**eet me at my house at nine tonight," said Lenny. "We're going to a party."

"Where we going?" I asked. With my hearing friends, I preferred parties that were close by. This allowed the Lone Deaf Guy to bail out and go home if things got too boring.

"The Cricket Club."

"Get out of here. Since when are we allowed in there?"

The Philadelphia Cricket Club is one of the most high class, fancy-schmancy places you could find in Philadelphia. They'd put Queen Elizabeth on a waiting list before they'd let her in.

"We're not going *in* there," Lenny explained. "It's at the golf course."

"We're golfing in the dark?"

"No, you idiot. Keg party at the fourth hole."

"A keg party on a golf course? What is this, *Caddyshack?*"

Later that evening we hitched a ride with two other friends and soon it became evident that this party was a great idea. The fourth hole was the perfect gathering place for teenagers. The green was at the bottom of a downward slope, and it was surrounded by trees. The isolated location pretty much ensured we could party all night and no one would see us.

I sighed contentedly as I sipped my drink. Nice, breezy summer evening. Nice, cold beer. It doesn't get any better than that.

Except that it was kind of dark. What the hell was everyone saying? It didn't take long for me to realize this was a lipreader's nightmare.

My eyes took a while to grow accustomed to the darkness. The moonlight helped a little, but it was going to be a bigger effort to communicate with anyone. Ah, what the hell. Time to schmooze.

"Hey, Jim!"

"What's up, Mark?"

"Good to see ya."

"How you doing?"

"Same old, same old. Just here to drink. Cheers."

"Cheers."

That went well. On to the next one.

"Hey, Dave!"

"Yo."

"How you doing?"

"Great. Good to see ya."

"Good to see ya."

Next!

"Hey, Chuck!"

"Hi, Mark."

"How's it hanging?"

"To the left, as usual. Good to see ya."

"Good to see ya."

Was I circulating, or what?

"Hey, Frank! How ya doing?"

"Good, dude. How you been?"

"Been working out. Lifting twelve ounces at a time."

"I'll drink to that."

See that? I'm a freaking socialite.

"Hey, Anthony! How you doing?"

"Hi, Mark. Good to see ya."

"Good to see ya."

All right, that's enough individual schmoozing. Let's move on to groups.

"Hey, y'all. What's up?"

"Hi Mark. Sgdjhsy dshshkhdys dhsjk djkskst dhskstd blah blah blah shskdhs dhhes hske gsjet dhsiey dhskksy ddywqsj ksjdlcn shdkpl ldhsy shwqq kjs dhjbn shdywt."

Uh, forget about groups.

"Pete! How you doing?"

"Hi, Mark."

"Good to see ya."

"Good to see ya."

See the pattern?

I engaged in what's called social bluffing. As you could see in the dialogue above, this involves one superficial conversation after the other. Sometimes, as deaf as I was, I'd actually dominate a conversation. This is a common strategy for the hard of hearing conversationalist.

Note: My audiogram had long since nosedived to "profoundly deaf." But since I'm postlingually deaf, I've always had the ability to talk like a hard of hearing person. And sometimes I talk too much.

"Hey, Craig!"

"Yo, Mark."

"How you doing?"

"Good. What's up?"

"Not much. Hey, is there a porta-potty here? No way a deaf guy is going to piss in the woods. Did I ever tell you what happened at that deaf baseball game? There was this deaf baseball team that had an away game at Fairmount Park. There wasn't a toilet anywhere for miles. So of course, three players had to take a leak. When you gotta go, you gotta go, right? Well, the team van was parked all the way down the left field line. It was the only spot where they could take a whiz without being seen. So they ran behind the van and took a nice, long piss. While they were pissing, the umpire yelled at the driver to move the van away from the field. You see where this is going, right? Yeah. So the driver turns on the ignition. Three guys are pissing like there's no tomorrow and of course they can't hear the van start. Next thing you know, the van moves and suddenly there's these guys standing there with their pants down. Right there in front of all the spectators. It was awesome, man."

Look at it this way: If I'm doing all the talking and you're not, that creates a zero percent chance of me misunderstanding anything you say. Because I'm not allowing you to say anything! How brilliant is that?

Deaf and hard of hearing conversationalists can be master manipulators when the situation calls for it. It gives the illusion that we're doing just fine fitting in with the hearing folks. Often, friends and relatives will marvel at how well we adapt.

It's not "adapting." It's bullshitting.

Of course, it takes considerable effort to pull this off. There are plenty of moments where you get tired and need to take a break. In which case, there's only one thing to do:

Back to the keg I go!

After getting a refill at the keg, I made some small talk with a guy I'd never met before. And it so happened to be a guy who had perfect, easily lipreadable speech.

Hallelujah!

Every deaf person knows what I'm talking about. There's always that one rare bird out there who's easy to understand, and I was fortunate enough to find one at this party. Finally I could relax and have more of a

94

normal exchange with someone. Here's the gist of our conversation:

"Hey, I'm Mike. How ya doing?"

"I'm Mark. Nice to meet you. Great party!"

"It sure is! This is the perfect place to have a kegger."

"Yeah. For a moment there I was worried we'd get busted. But no one can see us down here."

"Oh, don't worry about that. My dad's a cop. He said no one would bother us."

Did this guy just say that somewhere out there, a policeman knew exactly what we were doing?

"Excuse me? Your dad's a cop and he's cool with this? Holy shit."

"Yeah. Awesome, isn't it?"

"I'm impressed. Great party, Mike." We shook hands and I went looking for Lenny. I found him near the woods talking to a few old friends.

"Lenny! Come here. I need to talk to you for a second."

"What's up?"

"That guy over there said his dad knows about this party. His dad's a cop."

"You have *got* to be kidding me. Are you sure he said that?"

"Positive. Keep your eyes open. You never know."

Lenny walked over to our friends, Jerry and Tony, and whispered in their ears. They nodded affirmatively. We had a plan in case the worst happened.

The worst happened.

Out of nowhere, three police cars slowly crept up at the top of the hill. They waited until the right moment and then turned on their sirens and floodlights.

Ambushed! Everybody run!

Lenny, Jerry, Tony, and I were already in position. We made a lateral escape into the woods while the police bore straight ahead and backed everyone else up.

As the police methodologically escorted underage party-goers off the premises, my friends and I patiently waited in the woods. Lenny and I had ducked for cover behind a tree. Jerry and Tony laid flat in a brush. We managed to avoid detection as the police canvassed the area.

Dare I say it, this was actually fun. I smiled and flashed the thumbs-up sign to Jerry and Tony. They reciprocated, pleased at how they had the last laugh.

They didn't. That brush where they ducked for cover? Poison ivy.

A few minutes later I wondered if the coast was clear. "Lenny?" I whispered. "Are the cops gone yet?"

"Shhh!"

I could see why Lenny wasn't happy with my timing. A policeman shined a flashlight in our direction. We held our breaths for ten very long seconds. The policeman moved on.

Whew. Crisis averted. But we still had a problem. We had to get out of there and we weren't sure how. There was a big chain link fence behind us and the police were still searching the area in front of us. Would we be able to make it over that fence without getting caught?

We took a good look at the fence and agreed it was our best option. We went ahead and scaled it as quietly as we could. Somehow we made it without drawing any attention to ourselves. Meanwhile, Jerry and Tony elected to stay where they were. They waited it out in their nice little cozy patch of poison ivy.

Once we hopped over the fence, Lenny and I found ourselves at the bottom of a dead-end street. The only way out was to walk uphill. Fine and dandy, but there was a police car parked at the top.

"We're fucked," I said, stating the obvious. "What do we do now?"

96

Lenny thought for a moment and then smiled. He pointed at our clothes. We had on those Adidas jogging suits that were so popular in the '80s.

"Hell, no, Lenny. You're crazy."

"It'll work. Follow me."

Lenny broke into a jog. I kept pace with him as we made our way up the top of the street.

Stay cool, stay cool, I thought to myself. *And for chrissakes, run in a straight line, you stupid drunk.*

We nonchalantly jogged past the police car and gave the police officer a friendly wave. He waved back and we jogged on without incident.

He fell for it! The policeman actually fell for it!

It's human nature to embellish a story with the passage of time. As the years went by, the fence grew ten feet taller and the gullible cop's IQ plummeted fifty points. We sure fooled him, didn't we?

We did not. The more I think about it, the more I recall how the police officer could not wipe a silly smirk off his face. He knew damn well what was going on. Apparently he admired our creativity and decided to reward us with a free pass. Only in Philadelphia.

Wallflower University

"D *ude!*" yelled Rob. "You've *got* to hook up."

"With what?" I asked. "It's 2:30 in the morning."

"Shit. You're gonna have to come with us." Rob nodded to our friend Matt and two girls they'd met earlier in the evening.

Aw, great. I'm the fifth wheel.

We were at the University of Delaware and a late-night party had just wrapped up. At any other party I'd call it an evening and go home. Unfortunately, home was an hour's drive away and we'd all had a bit too much to drink. Driving back to Philadelphia on I-95 was not an option. We'd have to stay the night in someone's dorm room.

There's nothing wrong with sleeping off a few beers before you drive home. But when it involves watching two of your buddies hooking up with some girls they met while you struck out (again) because you were the only deaf guy on the whole campus, that's a mighty big helping of Fuck My Life.

I followed Rob and Matt back to the dorm with their new gal pals. One of them shot me a *who the hell are you* glance. That was Rob's cue to go into damage control.

"Oh, this is Mark. He's deaf. He reads lips." The girl's eyes widened in shock. Or was it pity? Aw, crap.

"Hi," she said. "It's... nice... to... meet... you."

"Nice to meet you, too."

Kill me now, will ya?

Both of the girls eventually learned how to talk in such a way that I could understand them. But it only worked when they spoke directly to me. When they were engaged in a group conversation with my friends, I couldn't keep up.

They talked and talked for what felt like several hours. I glanced at the clock and prayed for sunrise. It was only 2:55 a.m. I tried to catch a few winks on the floor but just couldn't get comfortable.

So this is why they named that movie "From Here to Eternity." Watching these lovebirds chirp all night felt like an eternity.

Morning finally arrived. Everyone said their goodbyes and then Rob, Matt, and I hopped into my car.

"Dude," said Rob. "I'm *so* sorry." I nodded my head and said it wasn't a big deal. It happens. Nonetheless, I appreciated the apology.

Two years later, the tables were turned.

The Night From Hell in Delaware was one of the last straws that motivated me to enroll at Gallaudet University. In the fall of 1989 I was finally a student in a school—and living in a dorm—where everyone signed. The difference was like night and day.

As fate would have it, my hearing friends visited for a weekend at Gallaudet. They were in for a rude wakeup call.

I can't imagine what it must have felt like for them to step onto a campus where just about everyone was deaf. No, wait. Who am I kidding? I can imagine what it must have felt like. Prior to attending Gallaudet, I'd gone to countless parties with thousands of hearing people.

99

After meeting up with my roommate and a couple of close friends, my hearing pals and I hung out for a while in Peet Hall. I'd brought some of my Gallaudet buddies back to Philadelphia for a weekend visit before, so my hearing friends were already comfortable with them. But as for the rest of the campus? It was overwhelming.

See where I'm going with this?

My girlfriend Melanie brought a couple of her friends downstairs to say hi.

Did I say "girlfriend?" Yes, I did. Finally. For a great majority of my time in the hearing world, I was a wallflower who struck out on a consistent basis. See what happens when a deaf guy gets to go to a school where it's a level playing field? Ask my girlfriend, uh, my wife, Melanie.

Melanie's friends were rather attractive. It didn't take long for my hearing buddies to notice. They quickly went into the old hook-up mode I'd seen so many times before.

Only this time, they struck out. Most deaf girls aren't that impressed with hearing guys who don't sign.

Matt tried his best to flirt with Lisa, a nice-looking brunette. But Matt's signing skills were next to nil, and Lisa made it clear she had no interest in someone who could barely communicate.

"Oh, it's sign language you want?" Matt retorted. "I can do that."

What followed was the most shocking display of *Pick-up Lines Gone Horribly Wrong*. Although Matt couldn't put together a coherent sentence in ASL, he knew his share of cuss words. Any hearing guy who has a deaf friend manages to pick up the more colorful vocabulary. Matt was no different.

"Shit. Fuck. Asshole."

Not only did Matt sign this to an attractive coed he just met, he did it with gusto. He was actually proud of himself.

100

"You're a pig, you know that?" Lisa shot back. "If that's all you can sign, I'm not interested."

For once, Matt was speechless. His plan wasn't working.

Well, duh. Can you imagine if, at the University of Delaware, I walked up to hearing women and voiced "Shit-fuck-asshole?" They'd have thrown my deaf potty mouth in jail.

Matt was clearly deflated. He'd assumed that just because he could hear, deaf women would view him as more desirable. Because, you know, deaf people are *handicapped*, and hearing people are not. Therefore, deaf women should be fawning all over the first hearing guy they meet.

You could see the realization sinking in. At that moment, Matt—and Rob—suddenly saw deaf people for who they really are. Not a group of handicapped people, but a vibrant community with its own language and culture.

Matt, Rob, and all of my other hearing friends never actually looked down on me. They always welcomed me to hang out with them back home. It's just that they may have subconsciously looked at the deaf community as something "special," something the hearing world was "better" than. That day in Peet Hall, Matt and Rob threw out "special" and replaced it with "different." As in deaf people are the same as anyone else, but with a different language and culture. And if you want to score with some hot coeds, you better know the language.

Matt shook his head and smiled as Lisa got up to leave.

"Have a good time at the party tonight," Lisa grinned. "Try to behave."

That's when Matt turned to me and said something I'd been waiting to hear for a long time.

"Dude," he said. "Now I understand how you feel with us back home."

Mr. Potato Head

Most of the anecdotes in this book are for the purpose of revealing how ignorant I was in the mainstream. Without a good frame of reference, it was hard for me to understand what I missed out on in the deaf world. Perhaps these stories will save someone else from a similar headache.

There's one caveat, though. I don't want readers to come to a black-and-white conclusion:

Deaf people are cool! Hearing people suck!

It took me twenty-three years to fully assimilate into the deaf community and truly get it. There's a reason it took so long.

Hearing people don't always suck.

It's not like I suffered through every waking moment. I grew up with the most awesome friends a guy could ask for. I met most of my childhood friends either on the baseball field or at a local swim club, and our friendship would last through the college years and beyond. Even if my ability to keep up with their conversation took a nosedive in later years, they always went out of their way to include me. I love my buddies. Individually, each and every one of them is a great friend. As a group, it was inevitable that I'd spend long stretches as a wallflower. It is what it is.

Just the same, there were many good times with my hearing friends. We played baseball and softball. We hung out at the beach. We had lots of memorable moments. I would like to share one of those moments just to point out that hearing people do not, in fact, totally suck.

During the late '80s I played softball for Towey's Tavern. There was one year—I can't remember which one because it was a bar league, for chrissakes—when I had a good feeling about our team. We had just won our season opener and were celebrating at Towey's.

"Lenny," I said, in between sips of a nice cold beer. "I think we're going to win it all this year."

"You and me both," Lenny replied, as we toasted the upcoming season.

"In fact," I added, "I'm going to make a guarantee. If we win the championship, I'll drink out of my jockstrap."

"I'll do you one better," Lenny smiled. "If we win, I'll run up Germantown Avenue in mine."

"You're on, bro."

Long story short: We won the championship.

Three months later, we were back in Towey's Tavern as we celebrated our big win.

"Yo, Lenny!" I screamed over the din. "Watch this!"

I reached into my baseball pants and pulled the protective cup out of my jockstrap. A loud cheer went up at the bar. Everyone knew the deal. It was time to drink from the Holy Grail.

A teammate poured beer into the cup and I did what I had to do. What followed was the first standing ovation I'd ever had as a ballplayer.

For those of you who may be a bit squeamish, I'd like to point out that at no time during these theatrics did my protective cup ever come into direct contact with

103

my junk. Jockstraps have this separate compartment where you put in the cup. And yes, I washed the cup beforehand anyway. Just thought you'd like to know.

As the applause died down, everyone's eyes turned towards Lenny.

"I know, I know," Lenny acknowledged. "We're not done yet."

Lenny disappeared into the men's room. Three minutes later the ugliest sight emerged: Lenny wearing nothing but sneakers and a jockstrap.

For those of you who are still not familiar with the inner workings of the jockstrap, it consists of a protective covering in the front and the equivalent of two G-strings in the back. Yes, we could see Lenny's ugly bare ass.

Cheers erupted as Lenny prepared for his historic run up Germantown Avenue. He was not, however, as stupid as he looked. He had three months to prepare for this.

He reached into his equipment bag and pulled out a Mr. Potato Head mask.

"What?" he asked, in response to several puzzled looks. "You think I'm going to let anyone see my face?"

Turns out he really did think this out carefully. He didn't want any witnesses to be able to describe him to the police.

"Here's the deal," Lenny continued. "I'll run up the avenue. You guys follow me in the car. Pick me up at the top of the hill. If you see any cops, make a quick right and I'll jump in with you guys. Take my clothes with you just in case."

Lenny donned his Mr. Potato Head mask and gave a triumphant wave. Everyone raised a glass in his honor. It was truly a hero's send-off. You'd think we were sending Lenny to the moon.

Three teammates joined me in my car. As I started the engine, we gave Lenny the thumbs up. Lenny nodded and broke into a light jog. I gave him a twenty-second head start before following him up the avenue.

I was not—I repeat, NOT driving under the influence. I'd only had a jockstrap's worth of beer. If you knew the size of my jockstrap, you'd know that's not much. But I could not drive in a straight line. My teammates and I were laughing so hard we couldn't breathe. As Lenny's butt jiggled under the street lights, I wiped the tears off my face and focused on the road the best that I could.

It wasn't long before Lenny created a scene. As he approached Rosebud's, a quaint little café, he tapped on the huge picture window and jumped up and down.

Ooga-booga! Ooga-booga!

A couple of patrons were startled out of their seats. Other patrons actually applauded. Lenny saluted them and went on his way. I damn near ran off the road.

"I need a paper bag," I joked to my teammates. "That son of a bitch is making me hyperventil—oh, shit! Cops!"

Sure enough, just as Lenny had anticipated, a police car made its way down the opposite side of the avenue. Lenny promptly disappeared around the next block. I made a quick right turn and pulled over. Lenny jumped in and soon he was fully clothed.

As we made our way around the block and headed towards Towey's, we passed the policeman going back up in the other direction. Clearly he was driving up the avenue in search of Mr. Potato Head. He made a few more passes up and down the block, but Lenny had long since returned to a rousing welcome at the bar. The policeman gave up and drove across town to Dunkin Donuts for a cup of coffee at the end of his shift.

How do I know the policeman went to Dunkin Donuts, you ask? Because Lenny's mother worked there that night. The exasperated cop vented to her about how our society is going to hell in a handbasket.

"What's wrong with kids these days?" the policeman lamented. "No one's got any moral values. This idiot ran up the avenue wearing nothing but a jockstrap and a Mr. Potato Head mask. You could see his shiny white ass in the lights. Ugly as hell."

Lenny's mom shook her head in disbelief as she poured the cop a cup of coffee.

The next day, Lenny's mom dropped her car off at the shop for repairs. Lenny picked her up and gave her a ride home.

"You hear what happened on the avenue last night?" Lenny's mom asked.

"No, what?" Lenny shifted nervously in his seat.

"There was a streaker. Ran up the avenue wearing a Mr. Potato Head mask and not much else."

"Really?" Lenny shook his head. "Wow. I was at Towey's. Didn't hear anything about it."

"It's disgusting. A pervert like that ought to be locked up and..."

At that moment Lenny's mom felt something under the seat brush against her foot. She pulled it out and found herself staring directly at a Mr. Potato Head mask.

Yes, this is the kind of trouble my buddies got into. I'm honored to be their friend.

Super Phony

The phone suddenly rang in my office, snapping me out of a paperwork-induced fog. It was 2:30 p.m. on an otherwise uneventful Monday afternoon. The administrative secretary was on the line with an unexpected surprise. I jumped out of my seat when she told me that Cindy, a former high school classmate, was in the headmaster's office. I hadn't seen her in fifteen years.

Cindy was in town for the class of 1984's fifteenth reunion, which I had skipped. She was staying in Philadelphia for an extra day and thought she'd surprise me at work.

I rushed over to the administration building with much excitement and anticipation. This was a dear friend, one of a handful of students in my class who put in the effort to learn sign language. I was the only deaf student in the whole school and really appreciated her being sensitive to my communication needs.

As a matter of fact—I won't deny this—there was a time when I had a bit of a crush on Cindy in high school. I never really did anything about it, partly due to lack of confidence and partly due to not wanting to mess up a rare good friendship. After all, Cindy was one of few people who could really communicate with me.

And there we were, reunited once more, fifteen years later. I was in awe as we as we greeted each other in the headmaster's office. She was still an attractive and dynamic woman. In fact, more so than ever before; she was now *Doctor* Cindy, having earned her Ph. D. in veterinary medicine. And she also...

Whack!

Ouch. That was my wife Melanie bashing me on the head with a roller pin. Quit slobbering and get to the point, she says. And the point is, it was awesome seeing Cindy again. I was thrilled to catch up on the news with this very fascinating person. But something was different. In fact, in my mind I asked myself one question:

What the hell was I thinking?

As impressed as I was with who Cindy had become, and as happy as I was to see her, I realized we were as romantically compatible as oil and water. It had always been that way. Don't get me wrong, it's irrelevant anyway. I've been happily married to Melanie since 1994 and there is no one else remotely close in the way she is able to relate to me. Nonetheless, the question still perturbed me:

What the hell was I thinking?

I was completely taken aback at how my perspective had changed since those good old high school days. In 1984, I worshipped the ground Cindy walked on. Hey, she could sign a bit, she could *communicate*. Compared to the four hundred or so other girls who couldn't sign at all, Cindy was a goddess.

Fifteen years later, Cindy still has some signing skills, for which I'm grateful. Nonetheless, things have changed significantly ever since I've become a member of the deaf community. Today I'm very comfortable in the presence of others who sign ASL fluently. Especially my wife, Melanie, roller pin and all.

And that's what struck me so hard. In 1984, when few people in my world signed, Cindy was *the bomb*. She set a standard no other girl in the school could match. But in 1999, it was a different story.

As we talked in my office, I could only lipread about fifty percent of what she said. Her signing skills—actually, her finger spelling skills, to be honest—added perhaps another thirty percent. The rest was purely fill-in-the-blanks guesswork on my part. It did take some effort, especially the lipreading.

What the hell was I thinking?

It really bothered me because I had stumbled across a sobering truth. In 1984, in my valiant effort to fit in with the mainstream, I was totally full of shit. I was Super Phony. Telling the whole world, *hey, this is cool, I can fit in*. Telling everyone *hey, don't worry, I communicate just fine with my hearing classmates*. Who was I kidding?

This is really nothing new. In previous writings I've pointed out how I insisted I fit in just fine with my hearing baseball teams. Yet when I joined the Gallaudet baseball team years later, I realized there was simply no comparison. With the Gallaudet team I could not only communicate with my deaf teammates significantly more during the actual games, but also in the locker room and on road trips.

With the aforementioned hearing teams, so many people marveled at how this brave deaf boy was able to fit in. Oh, please. I might have fit in on the field. But on the bench, in the locker room, and on the team bus, I was still Super Phony. In Cindy's case, I didn't realize it until just now: Super Phony had struck once again.

It's an easy-to-overlook social phenomenon that affects anyone who's ever been mainstreamed. It's the *"Hey Ma, I fit in just fine with the hearing folk"* lie that we often tell ourselves.

At first glance, many deaf people, myself included, are able to make it in the mainstream. We do it with smoke-and-mirrors fake smiles and lots of nodding. Often we're reinforced by well-meaning parents and teachers who gush over how well we appear to assimilate. They're thrilled if we learn our ABCs, but oblivious to the social isolation we deal with. Regardless, in the midst of their own excitement they'll continue to unload lavish amounts of praise.

"Oh, he speaks so well, he's just like any normal hearing person!"

The sad thing is many of us actually believe it, especially when we don't have a frame of reference. Which is why in 1984 I would have considered having ten children with Cindy, while today I understand she's a dear friend who, in spite of her many fine qualities, doesn't even come close to what Melanie has to offer.

There are countless other Super Phonies out there. Some may feel comfortable getting by in their environments. Others may look back and say the same thing I said:

What the hell was I thinking?

And when they say that, I'll only smile and welcome them—just like the deaf community did for me.

Tuning Out

"**W**ere you having a side conversation?"

"Um, no. We were…"

We were busted.

My good friend and co-worker, Patty, was with me at an educational workshop that had gone stale. The guest speaker droned on in a monotone and everyone in attendance was comatose. It was impossible for anyone to stay focused. So sue me, Patty and I did indeed have a side conversation.

It was right before lunch break when one of the event coordinators approached us. As tactfully as possible, he let us know that our side conversation was inappropriate.

That's right. We're deaf professionals in our forties and we got called out for our behavior. We felt like delinquent high school students.

"I don't mean to intrude," the guy said. "But it was brought to my attention that your signing is distracting for some of the people here."

"We were talking about some of the points the presenter made," Patty responded. "Some of the things she said apply to situations we deal with at our school."

Well, yeah. Some of our conversation was work-related. But for the most part, we talked about how much we looked forward to Deaf Professionals Happy Hour.

"Oh, that's perfectly understandable," the man replied. "I'm just passing along what others have said."

"We can move to the back of the room," Patty offered.

"No, no, you don't have to do that. I'm just letting you know so you're aware of it."

At that point a woman who was sitting next to us intervened.

"I don't find the sign language distracting at all," she said.

And she was right. If the sign language was so distracting, they would've asked the interpreters to leave.

The event coordinator smiled and left. Patty and I stared at each other in disbelief. We sighed and left for our lunch break. But this wasn't over yet. We saw the event coordinator down the hall talking to our interpreter about our behavior.

Oh, no! He's telling mommy on us!

Patty and I had to go down the hall and bail out the interpreter. For chrissakes, it's not the interpreter's job to keep us in line. We had to make sure that the guy understood that it was us, not the interpreter, who dictated what was going on.

The interpreter made a nice comment about how "ASL is interactive" before I was able to jump in. I remarked that ASL is indeed eye-catching so it would be no problem for us to move to the back of the room. Again, we were told that was not necessary.

All right. Let's cut to the chase. Yes, Patty and I had a side conversation and we got busted. But before you send us to our rooms without supper, consider what the hearing people in attendance were doing:

Exhibit A: A woman sitting near us read and replied to emails throughout the duration of the workshop (attendees were permitted to bring their laptops). I guarantee you her typing is louder than my signing.

Exhibit B: Another lady browsed through Facebook on her laptop while the guy next to her played solitaire on his.

Exhibit C: Several people got up and left the room in between the allotted break times.

Exhibit D: The man sitting behind me fell asleep. I guarantee you his snoring is louder than my signing.

Exhibit E: Several people packed their bags, put their jackets on, and walked out of the workshop a good fifteen minutes before it was over.

Exhibit F: Numerous hearing people whispered to each other and laughed. I guarantee you... ah, hell, you get my drift.

All of these people were clearly not engaged in the workshop and it was okay. But when the two deaf people in attendance stepped out of line, someone had to do an intervention.

This is nothing new. It's been going on for years and it's not limited to deaf people in the hearing world. In fact, I think it might be worse in the deaf world. Go to any staff meeting at a deaf school and you'll see that hearing employees get away with whispering to each other all the time. Meanwhile, deaf people who sign to each other often get called out. I've seen speakers on stage (hearing and deaf speakers alike) stop what they're doing to publicly reprimand the deaf offenders.

I bring this up because in the mainstream, countless deaf children face the same unwanted attention. They're constantly reminded to sit up front and keep their eyes on the teacher or interpreter at all times.

I remember the last time someone was required to pay one hundred percent attention. It was in a movie called Clockwork Orange.

113

During my own presentation—where people are more than welcome to have side conversations and walk out—I'd got into the habit of saying that the ASL interpreter at my high school gave me one hundred percent access. I said this because it felt like the floodgates to unlimited information had opened on the first day I had an interpreter. I immediately knew I had exponentially more access in lectures and class discussions compared to the days when I had to sit up front and read lips on my own. But *one hundred percent?* No way.

No one gets one hundred percent. Not even the hearing folks. Hearing people daydream, scribble in their notebooks, check their email, and take unnecessary bathroom breaks. Deaf people have the right to do the same. In fact, we need it even more. It's mentally and physically draining to have our eyes glued to the wiggling fingers of an interpreter all day long.

Ask any kid in the mainstream how he or she feels about being reminded to sit up front and pay attention. My kid kvetches about it all the time.

Tuning out is a skill that has its own benefits. It's a release valve that allows you to cope with boredom and exhaustion. It teaches you how to fill in the blanks when you need to catch up on material you missed. And if you do indeed miss out on important information, that's a natural consequence that teaches you how to be responsible for what you need to know.

Natural consequences are good for you, folks. Too many deaf children are spoon-fed in school. If they don't experience natural consequences, they'll never be prepared for that cold, cruel world out there after they graduate.

Bottom line: We all reserve the right to take a mental break when we need one.

114

The Truth Shall
Set You Free

After my son Darren's first year at Camp Mark Seven—his first all-deaf overnight camp—he said he had an awesome time. However, he was only ten years old back then so when I asked him if he was ready for an all-deaf school, he wasn't fully sold on the idea. He was born hearing and still had several hearing friends with whom he'd grown up going to school with. Old habits die hard. Only when I asked him how he'd like it if his Camp Mark Seven friends were his classmates did he experience a paradigm shift. It was at that moment when he realized school could be a lot more fun than it actually was.

After Darren's fourth camp session at Camp Mark Seven, there was absolutely no doubt about it. Prior to camp, Darren had finished his first year as a mainstreamed middle school student. In elementary school, a great deal of Darren's interaction with other students was play-based; in middle school, teenagers basically talk and hang out. Seventh grade was a different world and a much more frustrating one at that. So to return to Camp Mark Seven and interact with deaf peers who could communicate effortlessly with each other was a breath of fresh air. And finally, as a thirteen-year-old, Darren knew what he wanted.

"I don't want to go back to Pennbrook," he said, as soon as he got in the car. "I've had enough of being left out."

"You don't have any friends at Pennbrook?" I asked.

"Sort of. The baseball team is fun and I have Pennbrook friends on Facebook. But in class and in the cafeteria I'm on my own. At a deaf school I could be friends with anyone."

The kid was right. And this was a heart-wrenching discussion for his parents. For as much as Melanie and I agreed with him, finding a deaf school that met his needs was going to be tough. What with the economy being in the toilet and all, it's not that easy to uproot the whole family, find new jobs, and buy a house near the Ideal School for the Deaf.

Almost all deaf schools require you live in the state where they are located. The only exception is the Model Secondary School for the Deaf, a federally-funded program where deaf students from all over the country can go. But MSSD is for grades 9-12, and Darren was just about to enter the eighth grade. One more year of purgatory to go. Needless to say, Darren was pissed.

After we left the campgrounds, we went further north and our family enjoyed a road trip through Montreal, Toronto, Niagara Falls, and Rochester. Rochester was Darren's idea. He wanted to visit two of his friends who attended Camp Mark Seven a few years ago. One of those friends was home and we had a nice visit, but the other one was at a summer program at the Rochester School for the Deaf. Fortunately, the father of this friend happened to work at RSD and he was able to arrange for a last-minute school tour.

During our visit at RSD, our tour guide brought us into an eighth grade summer school class, where Darren was surprised to find one of his friends from Camp Mark Seven. Their conversation started like this:

"Sam!"

"Darren! What are you doing here?"

"Just visiting with my family."

"Are you going to go to school here?"

"I hope so. I want to."

From there, Darren's friend introduced him to the other students and they talked for a good twenty minutes. Every now and then, Darren said something funny and everyone laughed. They exchanged text numbers and email addresses. They hugged when it was time to leave.

That's when it hit me. In twenty minutes, Darren had made more friends and engaged in more conversation than he'd done all year at Pennbrook. This is what he was talking about a few months earlier when he said he was tired of being a follower and wanted to be a leader.

The ride home was a reality check. Darren didn't know that in order for him to be a student at RSD, we had to live in New York. He was crushed when we explained this to him. He wanted Rochester and he wanted it *now*. His spirits lifted somewhat when we promised him that if we couldn't make a move to Rochester, there was always MSSD. That was my plan all along—for his high school years, Darren would go to a deaf school. That he ran out of patience in the seventh grade was no surprise and, in fact, totally understandable.

"We'll see what happens," I assured Darren. "One way or the other, you *will* wind up going to a deaf school. But just to be sure about RSD—you do know they don't have a baseball team, right? And Rochester gets ridiculously cold sometimes. Even if you play in a rec league, I don't think you'll play baseball as much as you do back home." Darren acknowledged this.

This is the kid who has played baseball with a tremendous amount of passion since he was five years old. He's played on numerous travel teams and is a die-hard fan of the Philadelphia Phillies. One time I asked him if he would trade his baseball ability for the ability to hear, and he immediately said no. And yet... he would trade in baseball for the opportunity to attend a deaf school.

Two weeks later, it was déjà vu all over again. Darren got the opportunity to visit MSSD in Washington, D.C. Once again, he ran into a former Camp Mark Seven friend in one of the classes and connected with several students. As we walked through the school gym, by chance we met the baseball coach.

This was the clincher. A deaf school, a deaf baseball team. A place to belong like no other.

As of this writing, Darren is prepared for one more year of madness in the mainstream. Given a choice, he'd rather be in a deaf school right now. Thankfully he has a growing group of deaf friends with whom he maintains regular contact with online and by videophone. They mean the world to him.

But what about his hearing friends, you ask?

Darren remains friends with his hearing classmates, although in a more limited manner. He'll exchange a *how-ya-doing* in person and swap some jokes via instant messages and Facebook. Baseball is a godsend—it allows him to connect with hearing kids on his school team, his summer travel team, and his Fall Ball rec team. Even if Darren doesn't say much in the dugout, the action on the field bonds him with his teammates. The mutual respect is there. Nonetheless, there are issues in the mainstream that still affect him. Few people notice. Check out the next chapter for a couple of insightful people who did.

118

From the Outside Looking In

In a seventh grade essay contest at St. Stanislaus School in Lansdale, PA, twelve-year-old Ryan McSorley took first place in the Inspirational Writing category. Ryan and his classmates had read Gary Kaschak's *The Hole to China* and their assignment was to compare the hero from the novel to a real-life hero.

The hero in *The Hole to China* was twelve-year-old Marty Kent. The real-life hero Ryan chose was twelve-year-old Darren Drolsbaugh. Yes, my little chip off the old block.

Ryan and Darren were baseball teammates for three years on the Montgomery Wolverines travel team. When they played in 10u and 11u, it wasn't a big deal that Darren was deaf. The coaches and players spoke a little more deliberately and used some visual-gestural communication when interacting with Darren. Other than that, it was baseball as usual.

In 12u, the team signed up for a week-long tournament at Cooperstown Dreams Park in upstate New York. This was one year after Darren had learned of—and come to greatly admire—the exploits of William Ellsworth "Dummy" Hoy.

Darren knew that Dummy Hoy was the first deaf baseball player to enjoy a long career in the major leagues. He also knew that the deaf community had been trying for years to get Hoy elected into the National Baseball Hall of Fame. So there was no way Darren was going to play a tournament in Cooperstown—right in the backyard of the Hall of Fame—without doing something to raise awareness for Dummy Hoy.

During the tournament, Darren had "Dummy Hoy" inscribed on his cleats and he played as if his hair was on fire. He went from home plate to second base on an RBI bunt single (alertly taking second base after the first baseman threw home) and triumphantly pointed at his cleats after the dust cleared. But the biggest accomplishment, for him, was writing a letter on behalf of Dummy Hoy and personally delivering it to the Hall of Fame.

The Wolverines accompanied Darren when he delivered the letter. Later on, Darren had the honor of a private meeting with Brad Horn, Senior Director of Communications and Education at the Hall of Fame.

Ryan was in awe as all of this unfolded. In his winning essay, he wrote that Darren's advocacy for Dummy Hoy at the Hall of Fame was a brave thing to do. However, he also duly noted what went on in the barracks at Cooperstown Dreams Park.

Most people are clueless about what it's like for a deaf person to be lost in the mainstream. Ryan is one of few hearing people—and definitely one of the youngest— insightful enough to see and understand what goes on in Darren's world.

I had already suspected that a week of bunking with hearing teammates might be frustrating for Darren. Hanging out with hearing teammates for a few hours is no problem; living with them for a whole week is another story. With that in mind, I allowed Darren to keep his cell phone with him and told him to text me as much as he wanted. As expected, he wound up texting me a lot. I knew it wasn't easy to be with non-signing teammates around the clock.

However, I still had no inside peek at what went on in the barracks at Cooperstown Dreams Park. Although Darren texted me often, he rarely complained (if he did, it was about the food). We pretty much talked baseball and that was it.

So when Ryan's parents sent me a copy of his essay, I was floored. Ryan was as brutally honest as he was remarkably insightful. Here's an excerpt where he compares Darren to *The Hole to China* hero Marty Kent:

"The players stayed in a small barrack for week. After a while, people started to get annoyed with Darren because he couldn't hear what they said or they tried to lip sync words to him and he didn't understand what they were trying to say. But later, they went and apologized to him and he forgave them. Marty was determined to dig his hole as far as he possibly could. Darren was determined to do what he loved, baseball. For both Marty and Darren they came upon rough and tough times but got through them despite their disadvantages."

It was interesting how Ryan saw more of what was going on than Darren did. Darren was so focused on the tournament, and so used to those awkward hearing moments, that he didn't fully realize how much of a struggle it was. Only later, after befriending several deaf kids at Camp Mark Seven, did Darren look back and say, "You know what? Being the only deaf kid for a week—that *was* tough."

It is this frame of reference—or lack of one—that impacts many deaf people, children and adults alike, in their quest towards self-realization. As I marveled at how

Ryan could understand what Darren went through more than Darren himself understood it, someone from my past popped up and gave me my own dose of the same medicine.

That would be Vicky Mitchell, my good friend who knew me both before and after I accepted my Deaf identity.

Vicky and I were students at Temple University in the late 1980s. She was one of few hearing people I knew back then who was fluent in ASL. We've stayed in touch over the years, and she always gets a kick out of telling my wife about the crazy things I did at Temple. Yes, she was there at that infamous *She Will Bite You* party. She'd seen it all. It doesn't bother me when she spills the beans to Melanie. Somehow it's a badge of honor. In fact, just before this book was published, I proudly showed Vicky a draft of the chapter featuring the party with the vampire wannabe.

And then Vicky threw me for a loop.

"Oh, yes, I remember that party," she reminisced. "You were so alone."

Excuse me? What was she talking about? This was the party where I hooked up with Kim, a crazed girl who had a strange affinity for vampires. Several guys warned me to stay away from her, but I went back to her room anyway because she could communicate in ASL. There was no way I was going to turn down a rare opportunity to connect with a woman I could actually communicate with. Okay, so I wound up regretting it immensely, but I was The Man. A legend amongst party animals.

"You were so alone," Vicky continued. "Just wandering around, not really talking to anyone."

Whoa. Paradigm shift. Vicky is a skilled ASL interpreter. When she signed *alone*, she held up a solitary finger and let it wander aimlessly in the air. To see her describe me that way in ASL was earth-shattering. I could feel the aloneness as if she put me in a time machine and took me back to a place where I didn't belong.

If you write "alone" on a piece of paper, it's just a word. If you sign it in ASL the way Vicky did, it's a visceral experience.

"Well, uh, yeah," I stammered. "It was hard to keep up with what was going on. That's why I outdrank everyone. I was real wild back then."

Vicky shook her head and looked at Melanie.

"He didn't know what he was doing," she continued. "I tried to tell him, but he wouldn't listen. He thought he was hearing."

Vicky was right. What in the world was I thinking back in those days?

The scary thing about this experience is the fact that I couldn't understand what Vicky tried to tell me until *after* I attended Gallaudet University. I needed the frame of reference before I could figure out what she meant.

"Damn," I said. "I didn't know it was that obvious. That's what I'm writing about in my book—mainstreamed kids have ways of convincing other people that they're fitting in. I was so good at it that I even fooled myself."

"You didn't fool me," Vicky replied. "I'd been around the deaf community long enough to know. But I can't force anyone to be deaf. You insisted you belonged in the hearing world so I had to respect that. I figured you would eventually find yourself. But you were so alone."

Have you ever had one of those moments were you suddenly *got it*, and realized that nothing really happened the way you thought it did? That your entire reality was, in fact, totally fake?

Whoosh! The rug was swept out from under me. The closest comparison I can come up with is Jim Carrey in

123

The Truman Show, a movie where Carrey's character—Truman Burbank—spent thirty years living in a fake reality. *I did this for twenty-three years. Not bad, eh?*

If I could do it all over again, I would never set foot in that Temple University dorm where Kim went Dracula on me. Not if I knew then what I know now. But back then? I was totally clueless.

Rarely did I think of myself as *alone*. In fact, when I first showed up, the first thing I thought was *whoa, this place is packed*. Never mind that I couldn't understand most of the conversation going on. The place was packed!

I must have said *how ya doing* to at least forty people. In my mind's eye, I was socializing. Never mind that my conversation rarely went beyond superficial. The place was packed! And all of those guys who said *how ya doing* right back at me had acknowledged my existence.

In a rare moment of self-awareness at that party, I felt awkward standing around by myself. So I grabbed a beer—again—and sat down next to a group of college coeds having a group conversation. They smiled, and I smiled right back. Once again, I interpreted it as validation that I belonged. Besides, the place was packed!

One of the coeds was Alicia, the cheerleader with whom I shared a platonic friendship that may or may not have turned into something more. We'll never know, because soon Kim showed up and all hell broke loose.

I spent several hours at that party before running out of there like a bat out of hell. Out of all those hours, there were only two brief instances where I acknowledged myself as *hopelessly lost deaf individual*: the moment when I felt awkward standing around by myself, and another moment when I questioned my ability to hold a conversation with Alicia. Other than that, I thought I did pretty well.

And then there was Vicky, all those years later, reminding me:

"You were so alone."

The more I think about it, the more I realize I was alone a lot more than I thought.

That other party at the University of Delaware? The one where I was stuck overnight in a dorm room with two couples slobbering all over each other? The dorm room was unbearable. But the party beforehand seemed just fine. In retrospect, the party was also unbearable. I just didn't know it. I allowed myself to be distracted by the blaring music, free-flowing alcohol, one superficial "how ya doing'" after the other, and lots of people dancing. Hey, the place was packed! I smiled a lot and laughed when other people laughed. It was like I was living vicariously through other people's joy, without fully realizing that I wasn't really having that much fun. It was a survival skill, something I had trained myself to do. To this day, sometimes I still smile at other people even when I have no idea what they're talking about.

It's amazing how Vicky gave me a sobering reality check so many years after the fact. Ryan's essay about Darren did more of the same and brought everything full circle.

Sometimes, those of us who are solitaires in the mainstream are so lost that we don't even know it. Sometimes, we don't wake up until we meet deaf peers who share similar experiences. And sometimes, we need genuine friends like Ryan and Vicky to show us an eye-opening perspective from the outside looking in.

Breaking Point

"I'm worried about Darren," said Melanie, texting me at work. "He flipped on his way to the bus. Cursed a lot and didn't want to go to school. Said he hates middle school and threw his backpack across the yard."

"That's not like him," I replied. "What exactly did he say?"

Melanie ran off a list of expletives that would have made George Carlin proud.

"Holy crap. I'll go get him. Call the school and tell them I'm on my way."

When I reached the principal's office, Darren was already seated next to the administrative secretary. She had me fill out an early departure form that asked for the reason Darren had to leave. It took every ounce of restraint not to write *because he's fucking tired of being the only deaf kid.* Instead I wrote a vague "family emergency."

"C'mon, Darren." I motioned to the door. "Time to go home."

As we left the building, Darren started to apologize.

"I'm sorry," he said. "I kind of lost it this morning."

"Not your fault," I replied. "It's mainstreaming. You've put up with it all year. I'm surprised you made it this far without snapping."

"I just couldn't take it anymore."

"It's all right. Been there myself. Hated it at my school, too."

At this point Darren was visibly relieved.

"Get me out of here."

"You got it. Let's go."

A smile. Darren felt better.

"Thanks. I thought I was in trouble."

"Nah. Your grades are good. You're on the honor roll. Your teachers love you. They keep telling me what a great sense of humor you have."

"But...?"

"But they'll never understand what you're going through. They're happy you're doing so well and I agree with them on that. They just don't know what it's like to be the only deaf kid."

"It sucks. I'm tired of being a stalker and not a leader."

"Stalker? You walking around with a chain saw and a mask?"

"You know what I mean. I shadow the other kids around the halls."

"You don't really talk to them, do you?"

"No. I sit with them at the cafeteria but don't say much."

"Fake smile?"

"Fake smile."

"Sucks. You want to tell your teachers or a counselor about this, or would you rather keep it private?"

"Private for now."

Darren had some good reasons he wanted to keep it private. He felt that ultimately he'd get referred for counseling, speech therapy, hearing aids, or maybe even a cochlear implant. Even worse, some staff might feel sorry for him and give him some unwanted extra attention.

"They'll make a big fuss over me," he reiterated. "I just want to be a leader."

"Just like at Camp Mark Seven, huh?"

"Exactly."

"All right. You're definitely going back to CM7 this summer. I assume you're also ready for a deaf school."

"Yeah."

"Okay. I get it. Mom gets it. We'll do the best we can. We're proud of you."

"What about the parents who don't get it?"

Damn good question.

One month later, Darren's younger brother Brandon had an interesting observation.

"Dad! You're not going to believe what happened at school today."

"What happened?"

"There's a deaf kid in the sixth grade. We had an assembly and he was crying."

This occurred at Brandon's elementary school, the same school Darren had attended the year before. A sixth grade class gave a performance as part of an anti-bullying program. Brandon's fourth grade class was in attendance.

"Are you sure he's deaf?"

"I'm very sure. He had hearing aids on."

"Why was he crying?"

"Everyone in the sixth grade had to take turns saying something. When it was his turn, he looked at the floor and mumbled. No one could understand him. He covered his face and later after that he started to cry."

"Did he have an interpreter?"

"No. Just hearing aids."

I wondered if this deaf student had any other issues that might have been a factor in preventing him from socializing with Darren.

"Does this kid seem to have any behavior problems?"

"No."

"Does he seem to be intellectually challenged or autistic?"

"No."

"Is he hard of hearing? Perhaps he speaks and hears a lot more than Darren?"

"No. He can't speak like Darren."

"He speaks even *less* than Darren and doesn't use sign language?"

"That's right."

"Oh, man, that's bad." I motioned for Darren to join the conversation. "Darren... at any time during the sixth grade last year, were you aware there was another deaf kid in the fifth grade?"

"No," said Darren, with a puzzled look.

"Geez. Let me see your yearbook from last year."

Darren got his old yearbook and Brandon looked through the fifth grade pictures.

"That's him," said Brandon.

"Oh, yeah, "Darren replied. "I've seen him in the hall. I don't know him but we walked past each other a lot."

"Did you know he was deaf?" I asked.

"No."

After sifting through some more yearbooks dating back to 2007, I discovered that this mystery deaf kid had been roaming the same halls as Darren for at least five years. And they never knew each other.

This was too much. How could this possibly happen? Was it ignorance? Were Darren and this other kid doing so well academically that everyone was satisfied with their success, but oblivious to other factors that make the mainstream experience stressful?

Or was it intentional? Was there some kind of *God forbid deaf kids meet other deaf kids* mindset at work here? No, I'm not being paranoid. Jaime Eustace-Tecklin, a deaf parent who has sent her kids to the same school, told me that she met the parents of yet another deaf student in the first grade. These parents had never met a deaf person until they met Jaime. They told her that their child's doctor encouraged them to avoid sign language at all costs.

The fact that this kind of thing still happens today absolutely boggles the mind.

When Jaime explained how much sign language had helped her succeed in school and in all other aspects of life, the parents were convinced. They've since enrolled in a sign language class and are enjoying a level of communication with their child that they didn't have before. But how many parents get such an opportunity to meet deaf role models? How many deaf children are drowning in isolation without this kind of access?

Note: What happened with the aforementioned deaf kids in the first and sixth grade was definitely not a reflection of the school they attended. I can tell you from experience that when Darren went there, the school bent over backwards to provide him with ASL interpreters, notetakers, and captioned videos. On top of that, they regularly provided ASL interpreters whenever my wife and I showed up for a meeting or school event. The incidents with the two other deaf students, in my opinion, are a reflection of the need to have deaf professionals involved with Early Hearing Detection and Intervention (EHDI). Too often, hearing parents of newly-identified deaf children are steered away from deaf-friendly options—without any input from actual deaf people who know a thing or two about growing up deaf in the mainstream. As a result, the goals that are agreed on at IEP meetings push deaf students deeper into a world of isolation. When I vented about this in an online discussion board, there was an interpreter who replied and said she once signed for Deaf Student A

*while being told to avoid eye contact with Deaf Student
B. Yes, this stuff actually happens.*

There was no way I could listen to Brandon tell me
what he saw and not do anything about it. I contacted
the school via email and tactfully explained what Brandon
had witnessed. If there was indeed a deaf child in the
sixth grade and he was indeed having a hard time, Darren
would be happy to visit and give the kid a pep talk. Darren
himself had attended a Gallaudet University baseball
game, I explained, and he met several of the deaf players
and coaches (including coach Curtis Pride, a deaf former
pro baseball player). The opportunity to meet deaf role
models playing the game he loves so much definitely had
a positive impact.

Understandably, for confidentiality reasons the school
could not disclose any further information. But they did
acknowledge they knew who I was talking about, and they
did say they would pass along my offer to the student's
parents. As of this writing I haven't heard anything from
them. It's heart-wrenching. To allow a deaf child to go
through his or her school years without access to deaf
peers and role models is sad. It's like a form of solitary
confinement.

Can you imagine putting an African-American student
in an all-white school and intentionally keeping him away
from other African-Americans? While you're at it, how
about separating all of the Asians, Latinos, and Indians?
That would be absurd, wouldn't it? But this is what's
happening with many deaf kids. Scares the hell out of me.
It's time for a change.

Part IV
Ending the Madness

How to Survive Mainstream School

Iit's been repeated at many a deaf education workshop that mainstreaming continues to be the primary option for most deaf and hard of hearing students. There's still this thing about *Least Restrictive Environment* and how it's interpreted.

To most people, *Least Restrictive Environment* means *make them fit in with the hearing kids as much as possible*. To me, LRE means *Legislators Ruined Everything*.

One thing legislators forget is that there's a big difference between *fitting in* and *belonging*. I've said this many times and it bears repeating:

Fitting in requires effort. It's exhausting and you can also argue that it's not genuine because it involves trying to win other people's approval.

Belonging is a far more rewarding phenomenon where you can kick back, be yourself, and know you are accepted. This is far more authentic and often happens in the presence of one's true peers.

Not enough people understand this. So if you're a deaf mainstreamed student and you're holding your own academically, you're not going to get much help in other areas that are just as important to your overall wellbeing.

With that in mind I've put together this list on *How to Survive Mainstream School*. It's based on actual techniques that have been utilized in the past. If you're a deaf mainstreamed student or you know someone who is, feel free to print these closely guarded secrets and use them as you see fit:

1. If you have a hearing aid, try your best to keep it concealed. The last thing you want is to look different.

2. During recess or lunch, hang out with a group of kids even if you don't understand them. Mimic their body language. Smile when they smile, laugh when they laugh. Pull off a few successful one-on-one conversations so that no one suspects you're totally lost in groups.

3. Agree wholeheartedly when adults marvel at how you "fit in just like any other normal kid."

4. Think like a secret agent. Search for clues in the library if there's something you missed in class. You can even recruit informants—trusted friends who know you can't hear. Check with them daily for lost information (homework assignments, special announcements, etc). But maintain a low profile and be careful not to blow your cover. Remember, you need to assimilate into the mainstream.

5. If a teacher asks you something and you don't understand, you can get away with asking him or her to repeat one time. If you misunderstand a

second time, it's best to shrug "I dunno" and be done with it. It's much better to look stupid than to look deaf. (There are plenty other stupid people in your school. How many other deaf people are there? Exactly.)

6. In gym class, always go to the back of the line whenever the teacher explains a new activity and you have no idea what he's talking about. This will buy you time to figure out what you have to do before it's your turn.

7. Be mindful that hearing people have a great affinity for music. It's very important to them and you're probably going to wind up in choir class sooner or later. You thus have two options: One, assimilate with the rebels by cutting class. You might wind up hanging out with the Goths or Stoners but the trade-off is worth it. Two, if you have any amount of residual hearing that allows you to pull this off, become an expert lip-syncher and Milli Vanilli your way through the Spring Concert. Yes, this is stupid. But remember, it's your job to fit in.

8. When you get home after a long day at school, act like a typical teenager when your parents ask how your day went: *"Fine."* Then go up to your room and give yourself a well-earned break. It takes an incredible amount of energy to fool people all day long. But it's all good—after all, you assimilated.

9. If rules 1 through 8 seem ridiculous, you're right. Ignore them and jump right to rules 10-12 if you want to make life easier.

137

10. Walk into your principal's office and tell him or her that it's insane to allow this charade to continue. Obtain a copy of Gina Oliva's *Alone in the Mainstream: A Deaf Woman Remembers Public School.* Give it to your principal and any of the people who insist you're "just like any other normal kid." Tell them straight-up: *This is exactly how I feel.*

11. Now you're in good position to request a sign language interpreter, assistive listening devices, a notetaker, and any other means of accessibility from which you stand to benefit the most. If this doesn't work, contact the nearest deaf advocacy group and have them vouch for you. If you have to fight for your rights, you shouldn't have to fight alone.

12. Speaking of not being alone, ask your school administrators: *Where are the other deaf kids?* You deserve to have friends who are just like you and understand what you're going through.

There you have it. I hope you enjoyed this list. If there's anything to be learned from it, it's the fact there's nothing wrong with being different. I prefer to call it being *unique.* It takes a lot of courage, I know. But a delightful new world opens up when you dare to be exactly who you are.

Parent Trap

Deaf people often enjoy my Deaf Again presentation because they find it validating. ASL students enjoy it as well because they find the language and culture fascinating. Parents, on the other hand, have a much wider range of reaction. Some of them love it because they're thrilled by the optimism and the opportunity for their deaf children. Others look like they just got off of a stomach-churning roller coaster. I don't blame them. The stuff I say is often at the far end of another extreme, far different from what others may have told them.

To all parents of deaf children: I don't know if there's any other phenomenon that results in parents being bombarded with so much conflicting information. I get it. If your child is deaf, you might as well lock yourself in the basement. You'll need to fight people off with a stick. Every Tom, Dick, and Harry will come at you with his own perspective on how to raise deaf children.

Most likely, right off the bat you'll have people encouraging you to look into hearing aids, speech therapy, and cochlear implants. You'll make many a visit to your friendly neighborhood audiologist. You might feel you need a degree from M.I.T. to decipher all of the audiograms and related information promoting the use of assistive listening devices.

If that's not overwhelming enough, sooner or later you'll encounter someone advocating on behalf of the cultural approach. This devastating hearing loss, people will tell you, is actually a blessing where your child gets to participate in a fascinating culture with its own language, ASL.

"Oh, nice," you might think to yourself. "Now I have to go out and learn an entirely new language just to communicate with my own child."

But wait!

There's more. You'll also encounter those who agree with the concept of sign language, but not ASL. They might offer their perspective that it's Signed Exact English (SEE), or any variation thereof, that might be more appropriate. Start off with SEE, and maybe move on to PSE (Pidgin Signed English). That should do it. Or, if you're into phonetics, Cued Speech might do the trick.

It's enough to make you scream, isn't it? If all of this is confusing enough for parents of deaf children, how do you think a young deaf child would feel when confronted with all of this? Exactly. It's mind-boggling.

And I haven't even gone into educational placement options, which is a whole new ballgame in itself. Although I'm talking about hearing parents of deaf children, educational placement is an aspect that also has *deaf* parents of deaf children up in arms over some very difficult choices.

There's a definite, ongoing buzz in the deaf community over which deaf schools are the best. Armed with this information, deaf parents may feel compelled to uproot their families and move closer to an educational program that best meets the needs of their deaf children. This can be a very tough choice because it may involve moving out of state or even across the country.

Some advocates may be so caught up in their own ideals that they may forget who they're dealing with. Namely, parents of deaf children who must make difficult choices that will affect them for the rest of their lives. Many of these parents have to make these choices while they are still going through a grieving process over their child's hearing loss.

It is for this reason I was motivated to write an article titled *You Deaf People* where I acknowledged that advocates everywhere need to be more sensitive to the needs of parents of deaf children. If you read it, you'll see how I learned a valuable lesson about deaf advocacy.

The bottom line: If your child is deaf, there's a simple way for you to find all of the answers you need. First, carefully review all of the options available to you. And then, step away. Step away from the people trying to sell their philosophy on you (including me, Mr. Deaf Culture).

Sooner or later you will be able to make a very well-informed decision. Sure, there are countless experts out there, but it's you—and only you—who is the expert at knowing your own child. You'll be able to make the best choice. The key is to find a methodology that matches your child as opposed to forcing your child to match a methodology. And by *best choice* I don't mean "pick one." There doesn't have to be a black-or-white answer. It's an option to wear a hearing aid *and* use sign language, for example. (Yes, I'm blunt about this. Anyone who says "my way or the highway" doesn't have your child's best interests at heart.)

Another critical aspect is to make sure your child understands that he or she is not alone. Allowing your child to interact with other deaf children and adults with similar backgrounds offers a sense of optimism and validation.

Earlier in this book I shared a quote from the article *Deafness: An Existential Interpretation* by Stanley Krippner and Harry Easton. It's an eye-opening quote that bears repeating:

If parents are not able to accept the fact that their child is deaf and continue to deny the implications of the deafness, the resulting effects on the child are to encourage his own denial and lack of authenticity. Such a child is thus unable to accept himself and his capacity to emerge or become a unique person is blocked. He lives an existential lie and becomes unable to relate to himself and to other deaf individuals and to the world in a genuine manner.

And this, I promise, is the most effective approach: Unconditional support from parents. It's an exciting journey when a deaf child develops a healthy deaf identity. Enjoy the ride.

If It Ain't Broke,
Don't Fix It

One of my best experiences as a school counselor was a collaboration with Lancaster-Lebanon Intermediate Unit 13 in 1998. Having been a solitaire in the mainstream myself, I was eager to see what, if anything, had changed.

When I last left Germantown Friends School in 1984, I had gone through the entire program without ever seeing another deaf student in class. Fourteen years later, LLIU 13 was a different story.

I don't have the exact numbers. But what I can tell you is that the IU had deaf and hard of hearing students scattered all over Lancaster County, Pennsylvania. Some of them were solitaires. Others attended mainstream schools together in small groups of three or four, attending regular classes with an interpreter. I also remember visiting a self-contained classroom with an entire class of deaf elementary school students. But regardless of where they went to school or whatever arrangements they had in the classroom, these kids had a special monthly treat.

There would be a gathering once a month at the IU building. Every deaf and hard of hearing kid from

143

every program was bussed there for two or more hours of quality interaction. There were games, activities, entertaining guest speakers, and presentations on topics related to guidance and self-advocacy. I was invited to attend these monthly gatherings as both a participant and as a presenter.

This experience remains the only time I personally witnessed an Intermediate Unit hitting a home run. And in this age of *he's doing just fine, he fits in just like any other normal hearing child,* we need more programs that are mindful of a deaf and hard of hearing child's overall wellbeing.

You had to be there to see how much it meant to the kids. It didn't matter if they were playing scrabble or attending a lecture on how to navigate an IEP meeting. They genuinely enjoyed each other's company.

I wish I could tell you this story has a happy ending. It doesn't. For whatever reason—budget cuts, I assume—the IU stopped busing the kids to their monthly event. They changed it to a monthly evening event where parents had to bring their kids. Not enough families got involved and eventually the numbers dwindled to the point where the monthly gatherings stopped entirely.

I don't know for sure what happened with the parents. Maybe they just didn't have the time. Maybe they weren't aware of how vital socialization with other deaf and hard of hearing peers was for their children. It's common for deaf and hard of hearing children to put up a facade and act like everything's fine in the mainstream, and unfortunately this allows the cycle of isolation and frustration to continue.

When you're the only deaf or hard of hearing kid in your school, you feel tremendous pressure to conform to the Hearing Way. You want to be like your hearing classmates. You earn approval from your hearing teachers and your hearing parents when you do well—which is great in some ways, but troubling in that it encourages you to continue with the facade. The only way the facade comes down is if you perform so poorly in school that you need to have your placement re-evaluated. It's a lose-lose situation because by the time you're finally sent to a deaf program, you're already significantly delayed in linguistic and academic development. Meanwhile, those who do well academically in the mainstream continue to suffer in silence.

Let's go further back in time to another Intermediate Unit program. Several of my deaf friends went to Plymouth Whitemarsh High School in Montgomery County, Pennsylvania. For your reading pleasure, here are their comments after I asked them the following question: *Could you tell me what it meant to you to have deaf and hard of hearing classmates at your school?*

From Colby Tecklin, Class of 1992: *The fact that I had a small Deaf culture around me gave me a sense of belonging.*

From Patrick Kilgallon, Class of 1992: *It meant that there was someone who was going through exactly what you went through as a deaf person. Your struggle was almost the same as the other deaf person.*

From Deb (Struebing) McNulty, Class of 1988: *I had a deaf classmate who accepted me for who I am regardless of my level of deafness. I felt more free to be myself.*

From Sarah (Ruth) McDevitt, Class of 1992: *I loved being around other kids who were like me and I loved knowing that I could be completely myself with them. I was just Sarah, not "that deaf kid."*

It clearly meant a lot to these people to have deaf and hard of hearing classmates. So how's that deaf program at Plyouth Whitemarsh doing today, by the way? Eh. It isn't there anymore.

But wait! We're not finished. So far we've looked at the benefits of mainstream programs that did the right thing for their deaf and hard of hearing students. What about an entirely deaf school?

I decided to look for people who went to deaf schools and ask them what their experience was like. Their responses were off the charts. It would take another book to adequately tell their stories. I hope someone writes one. For now, a condensed version of *Life in a Deaf School* will have to do:

From Dr. Don Grushkin, Model Secondary School for the Deaf, Class of 1981:

I was mainstreamed alone from kindergarten to seventh grade. I never had more than two or three kids at any one time that I could really call a "friend" at any of the public schools I attended, and during those years, the total number of my friends was less than the number of fingers on my hands.

When I entered middle school, I was bullied and made fun of, simply because I was so different. The abuse nearly drove me to a breakdown. I begged my parents to let me go to a school for the deaf (I vaguely knew they existed), reasoning that there, I would not get picked on because I was deaf, but because of whatever flaws in my personality. My parents did not want me to go, because they were afraid I would "lose my voice." But they finally saw that I was not in a good situation there, and let me go to the Model Secondary School for the Deaf.

I had a bit of trouble my first six months, primarily because I didn't know how to sign. Once I was able to sign at a basic conversational level, the other kids left me alone, and I was able to develop more friendships. After graduating in three years, I had more friends than

I could count on my fingers and toes. And by the way, I never "lost my voice!"

From Dr. Frank Lala, California School for the Deaf (Riverside), Class of 1969 (and author of *Counseling the Deaf Substance Abuser*):

As a deaf child of an addicted family I had a devastating blow from an unfortunate childhood. I had attended Hollywood High School (mainstream) and California School for the Deaf, Riverside (residential deaf school).

CSDR provided emotional, social and cognitive abilities that were crucial to realizing my human potential and identity. CSDR provided extracurricular activities, leadership opportunities, and mentoring by successful deaf and hard of hearing adult role and language models.

Personally, CSDR's environment became normal, healthy and placid. The teachers cared about our learning and the dormitory counselors advised and protected us. It was heaven—the only real home I had.

Jaime Eustace-Tecklin offers a unique perspective as she attended both a deaf school (New York School for the Deaf, also known as Fanwood) and a mainstream program (Woodlands High School) during her secondary school years. She graduated from NYSD-Fanwood in 1995. Here's how she compares the two programs:

Really, both schools were good programs. Woodlands offered some academically-challenging classes that were not available at Fanwood. I went to Woodlands with three other deaf students and we stayed together as much as possible. We benefitted from the extra academic work, but at the same time there were some things Fanwood provided that Woodlands couldn't.

147

In science lab at Woodlands, the four of us were always partners. We weren't comfortable with the other students and felt a little weird around them, so we stuck together every time there was a lab activity. At Fanwood, it didn't matter who we teamed up with. We could partner with anyone. The more we worked with other students, the more we realized that we could learn from each other as much as we could learn from the teacher.

There were also more opportunities for "the full experience" at Fanwood. I was prom queen at Fanwood. At Woodlands? That never would have happened. I also wasn't that much of an athlete but I got to be on the volleyball team at Fanwood. Woodlands? Never would have happened.

Lynette (Gouker) Mattiacci, who graduated from the Model Secondary School for the Deaf in 1998, offers a story that shows you can go home again. Lynette actually attended the Texas School for the Deaf up until the third grade before her family relocated. She bounced around a couple of mainstream programs before eventually transferring to MSSD in the tenth grade. As a result, she rediscovered a spark from her early days at TSD, a spark she had nearly forgotten:

Sending me to MSSD was the best thing my parents could have ever done for me. When I started MSSD, I was literally in culture shock. I had forgotten what it was like to have one hundred percent communication accessibility. Everywhere I looked, people were signing and I was in heaven.

I was an introvert that slowly became an extrovert. I learned more about who I actually was as a person because I could articulate my opinions, view points, and know that I was talking to fellow peers that understood my perspective as a Deaf person. I learned how to make friends all over again. I learned how to initiate and maintain a two-way conversation. I was a bit delayed in that aspect because I was so quiet while mainstreaming and when I did communicate with peers, it was only via paper and pencil or interpreter.

I learned how to embrace Deaf culture again. I walked down the hallway proudly, using sign language in public without feeling embarrassed. My Deaf identity was firmly established once again. I threw myself into every extracurricular I could—school plays, peer advisor, clubs, yearbook, sports, even class officer.

I actually did the same things I did while mainstreaming, but the feelings and experiences were completely different at MSSD. For instance, on my volleyball team, my coach signed—there was no need for three-way delayed conversations with an interpreter. All of my teammates signed, the fans signed, and I had complete language immersion. It was beautiful. I loved traveling with my MSSD athletics team to different schools for the deaf, visiting the campuses and meeting other deaf people. We didn't only play versus other schools for the deaf, but regular schools, and that made us feel proud. We were not isolating ourselves or being 'cliquish,' and we were actual athletic equals with other hearing peers.

The school performances I was involved in were grand productions with ASL specialists and ASL coaches. For the first time in my life, I was proud to use ASL on the stage. It's a beautiful language, and not something to be embarrassed of.

At MSSD, I was able to take AP classes and even took Gallaudet courses and earned college credits. I ultimately graduated as salutatorian. At MSSD, I felt "normal" and did not have to worry about communication barriers. I could be myself. The friends I had, I knew I had because of common interests, instead of because they wanted to learn ASL. I felt as if I was finally an equal.

Some people fit into the "better late than never" category. Carolmarie Colello technically never attended a deaf school, but thanks to exposure to the deaf community she was able to experience a homecoming of sorts:

During the ninth and tenth grades I was mainstreamed without an interpreter at Edward R. Morrow High School. I was forced to sit in the front row at each class. It took a long time to get used to it. I never felt like I could fit in.

In the eleventh and twelfth grades I had a sign language interpreter. This was a big improvement because at least I could understand what other people were talking about. But even with the interpreter, it still felt funny. It was difficult to participate in class discussion because I was always behind by a few seconds. By the time the interpreter relayed a teacher's question to me, someone else had already answered it or the teacher had already moved on to another topic.

The interpreter improved my access to information but social life was still a struggle. I got weird looks from the other students and I didn't participate in social events. The prom? Forget about it. I never went.

Eventually I met a deaf man and when we dated, he introduced me to a deaf world I never knew existed. I was so thrilled to meet other deaf people like me. We could communicate with each other on an equal level. Finally it was possible to have deep conversations and meaningful relationships with others. Actually I did have a group of hearing friends who I could hang out with in high school, but it took some effort to communicate with them. Gradually my hearing friends faded away and I came to understand that the deaf community was the place where I truly belonged.

Obviously, social life in a deaf school has a lot to offer. There's constant real-time interaction in the hallways, cafeteria, school trips, athletic events, theatre, study hall, dorms, and so on. This kind of interaction is just as important as the interaction that goes on in the classroom. I've seen so many former mainstreamed students at Gallaudet University wondering out loud why this level of interaction wasn't available in high school. Isn't it time for us to make sure these opportunities are there for the next generation of potential solitaires?

Some people might say, *"Oh, schools are not a place you go to socialize. Deaf students can socialize after they graduate."* I beg to differ. A healthy mix of friends, social events, and leadership opportunities play a key role in helping children—deaf and hearing alike—grow into well-rounded adults.

Deaf schools are a valuable resource. So are the rare mainstream programs that *get it* and find ways to provide quality interaction time for their deaf students. It saddens me to no end when such schools and programs have to fight an uphill battle to stay alive. We need to keep them open and provide their students with the enriching experiences they deserve.

151

Mythbusters

A book titled *Madness in the Mainstream* would be remiss if it didn't include some of the myths that fuel the madness. For whatever reason—be it ignorance or political agenda—there are myths floating around that disparage sign language, deaf schools, and the deaf community. Here are some of them:

Sign language will hurt your English.

No. Lack of language will hurt your English. If you spend your formative years unable to understand anything going on around you, that's when you wind up with serious language issues. Sign language itself does not sabotage anyone's English ability. In fact, Patricia Elizabeth Spencer and Mark Marschark's book, *Evidence-based Practice in Educating Deaf and Hard of Hearing Students,* says the same thing: "Skill in ASL does not interfere with development of English skills." Want good English? Have early access to language and read lots of books.

Sign language will ruin your speech.

Again, no. In a whole lifetime of interacting with the deaf community I have never seen anyone's speech

152

skills nosedive because he or she used sign language. No two deaf people are alike and you'll find a wide range of speech ability ranging from "very clear" to "totally unintelligible." It is what it is. For a frame of reference, check out reality shows such as *American Idol*. It's easy to see that some hearing people have beautiful singing voices while others simply don't. Similarly, there are deaf people who have excellent speech skills and deaf people who don't. The same goes for sign language; there are deaf people who sign fluently and others who don't. Either way, the use of speech and the use of sign language do not affect each other. There are deaf people who can speak *and* sign fluently, there are deaf people with *both* poor speech and poor signing skills, and there are deaf people with varying ability in each area. Sign language itself has nothing to do with the ability (or inability) to speak. The same way parents of hearing children have no qualms about enrolling their kids in Spanish, French, German, Italian, and other foreign language classes, parents of deaf children can view ASL as a welcome addition.

Deaf schools are isolated.

Quite the opposite. As you've seen in the numerous anecdotes in this book, it's the mainstream environment that can be extremely isolating for many deaf children. In deaf schools, deaf children benefit from one hundred percent communication accessibility in both the classroom and in their social lives. Leadership opportunities with their true peers provide them with a strong foundation of confidence and skills that they take with them into the world after they graduate. If you do some research, you'll find that there was a sharp rise in successful deaf professionals after sign language was once again allowed back into deaf schools.

Listening and speaking are the keys to success.

I'm going to let internationally-renowned deaf actor, producer and comedian CJ Jones take this one. With his permission, here's a quote he shared in the PBS documentary *Through Deaf Eyes*: "It's all about the knowledge. It's about the heart. It's about the ability... knowledge is the most powerful vehicle to success. Not the ears. Not speech." CJ's right. If you can't take his word for it, go to a National Association of the Deaf conference or a DeafNation Expo and take the time to meet deaf professionals and entrepreneurs at the exhibit booths. All of them are signers. Some of them can speak, some of them can't. Conclusion: The ability to speak was not the determining factor in their success.

Deaf schools offer a lesser-quality education.

Yes and no. Unfortunately, there are plenty of deaf schools that do not offer the same quality education as their neighboring mainstream schools. The reason for this is the dramatically increasing tendency of school districts to place deaf children in mainstream schools first. Only as a last resort—after deaf children *have already failed* in the mainstream—do they get an opportunity to go to a deaf school. Teachers thus have to take a step backward before they can go forward. They need to teach at the level where these students are before they can expect to show any improvement.

On top of all that, deaf children with additional disabilities and social-emotional, physical or linguistic issues are often immediately sent to deaf schools that are considered better-equipped to teach them. As a result you'll find lots of teachers of the deaf teaching a population that is significantly delayed. Take a good look at this from the inside and you'll find a ton of inspiring stories. You'll see that students other people may have given up on are actually learning and, in fact, overachieving. But from the outside looking in, you'll see a school that is still not up to par with its hearing counterparts. One look at standardized test scores and it's immediately obvious. This in turn may scare away parents of prospective students, and the downward spiral of deaf education continues. If you want to find a deaf school where deaf children are performing as close to age-appropriate level as possible, you'll need to do some homework to find one.

The deaf schools with the most challenging academic curriculums are the ones where parents insist on their school as a primary option for their children. These schools are the ones with a strong deaf community (including knowledgeable hearing parents who sign) behind them. Ask around and you'll find them. It's not unusual for parents in the know to uproot their families to move closer to such a school. This speaks volumes about its value. If only the world at large could see this.

You need to keep your deaf child away from other deaf people.

Why on earth would you want to do that? Everyone needs a role model. When African-American baseball players Jimmy Rollins and Ryan Howard rose to stardom with the Philadelphia Phillies—eventually winning a world championship in 2008—there was a sharp increase in African-American children playing baseball in Philadelphia. Likewise, why wouldn't anyone want deaf children to have deaf people to look up to and emulate? In *Deaf Again* I wrote about a self-imposed glass ceiling that held me back until I finally met some successful deaf adults. With that in mind I've made it a point to expose my deaf child to as many successful deaf people as possible. It gives him proof, knowledge, and confidence that deaf people can succeed in this world. Why would anyone want to shield a deaf child from this? It's insane. As much as possible, deaf children need to meet deaf peers and role models. It gives them all the more inspiration to say *hey, I can do this*. It doesn't matter if these deaf peers communicate differently or use varying forms of assistive technology (such as hearing aids and cochlear implants). In such instances, *hey, I can do this* becomes *hey, I can do this—in so many different ways.*

Deaf children with cochlear implants need to avoid sign language in order to enhance their listening and speaking skills.

Research has proven the exact opposite. It's been shown that signing prior to and after cochlear implantation *enhances* the development of spoken vocabulary instead of interfering with it (for more details, I refer you once again to Spencer and Marschark's *Evidence-based Practice in Educating Deaf and Hard of Hearing Students*). There was also a fascinating study by Dr. S. Hassanzadeh from the Iran Cochlear Implant Center, which revealed that second generation deaf children with cochlear implants (more specifically, deaf children from deaf families who had a strong language base in sign language prior to implantation) did better with their cochlear implants than implanted children from hearing families. Dr. Hassanzadeh, just like Dr. Spencer and Dr. Marschark, concluded that sign language helps children with cochlear implants acquire spoken language. It's becoming more and more evident that it's time to do away with the misguided belief of *keep the CI kids away from the signers.*

The more a deaf person can speak, the smarter he probably is.

Um, no. There are a lot of speaking idiots out there. Just because sound comes out of someone's mouth doesn't mean he has a brain (there are *plenty* of politicians who can prove this point for me, but I digress). It would be stereotyping at its worst to assume a correlation between speaking ability and intelligence. I have met so many people, both hearing and deaf, who can speak clearly yet are obviously a few sandwiches short of a picnic.

Conversely, there was a teacher at Gallaudet University who, as far as I can tell, doesn't speak. He was, however, very fluent in ASL. To this day he's the only person who got me to understand how a camera works. Anyone who knows me will tell you I'm extremely inept with technology. But thanks to this college professor and his classifier-rich ASL, I was actually able to comprehend the inner workings of a state-of-the-art camera. A couple of signs and I *got it.* Not one word was verbally spoken and this man opened my dense mind to the overwhelming world of modern technology. You get my drift. The spoken word is just one means of conveying and acquiring knowledge. There are plenty of other ways, so it's not wise to judge.

Deaf people who use sign language are isolated from society.

This myth is so prevalent that it warrants its own chapter. So I wrote one. Read on and enjoy.

157

The Isolation Myth

During Super Bowl XLII, a Pepsi commercial featured two signing deaf actors. This was awesome exposure because it showed a worldwide audience that culturally Deaf people lead normal lives and have a great sense of humor.

It wasn't long before the Alexander Graham Bell Association for the Deaf fired off a letter of protest to Pepsi. AG Bell, which prefers to endorse speaking and listening over sign language, insisted that the ad was misleading because a great majority of deaf people don't sign.

It's true that there are lots of people with varying degrees of hearing loss. Many of them consider themselves *hearing impaired* or *hard of hearing* rather than deaf. Within that category you'll find a significant number of people who don't know sign language. That's fine. I respect any deaf or hard of hearing person's individual communication preferences.

But there was one sentence in AG Bell's letter that threw me for a loop because it included the most overblown myth that's often used to discredit the signing deaf community. Check this out and try not to spew your coffee:

Your advertisement perpetuates a common myth that all people who are deaf can only communicate using sign language and are, therefore, isolated from the rest of society.

There you have it, the Greatest Myth of Them All: *Sign language isolates the deaf from the rest of society.* There is no way I can publish this book without addressing this extremely harmful fallacy.

First, let's soak in the irony.

You want to talk about isolation? I'll tell you that the seventh and eighth grades at Germantown Friends School were the most isolating years of my life. Those were the years I did not use sign language. I got by using my speech and listening skills. I was the poster child for oralism and I was lonely as hell. By the ninth grade, my teachers had seen enough. They got me a sign language interpreter and everything changed. ASL granted me more access to language and more access to learning. Some of my classmates were inspired to learn ASL when they saw its value. ASL, then, was clearly my bridge to the hearing world and not an isolating barrier.

Jump a generation ahead and you'll find my son Darren making similar comments. Of course, Darren and I are a small sample size. A dissident could easily say *that was just your experience.* My reply to that is *get yourself a copy of Gina Oliva and Linda Lytle's groundbreaking book,* Turning the Tide: Making Life Better for Deaf and Hard of Hearing Schoolchildren. *It's the most comprehensive book on the subject. Read it and you'll see very clearly that Darren and I are not the only ones who were isolated in the mainstream.*

You can attack the isolation myth from so many angles. How about this one: There are plenty of deaf people who sign *and* speak. They code-switch all the time. Who said sign language and speaking are mutually exclusive? There are deaf people who are adept at both ASL and spoken English. That's perfectly fine. Whatever works.

159

Then you have deaf people who sign but cannot speak. So is it this group that's isolated? No. They'll be the first to tell you they don't consider themselves to be at a disadvantage. This might seem odd to the average layperson. However, deaf people who have the empowering support of the deaf community usually don't fall into the trap of deficit thinking. It doesn't matter to them if they can speak or not. They find other ways to communicate be it through gesturing, pen and paper, text messaging, and so on.

A lot of times, through repeated interaction, hearing people are motivated to learn sign language. For example, there's a convenience store near my home where one of the employees is an ASL student. She signs when she greets my family and the other employees find it fascinating. Several of them have asked us how to sign certain words and phrases, and now they're surprising other deaf customers by greeting them in sign language. It's like an ongoing ASL club in there. That's not isolation, it's inspiration.

Granted, there are those who fear that the strong bond that exists within the signing deaf community results in its shutting everyone else out. The truth is, we can't shut anyone out. The hearing world is everywhere. We couldn't shut it out even if we wanted to.

I wrote about this in Anything But Silent *back in 2004. Not much has changed. Let's take an updated look at the same argument.*

Obviously I'm up to my eyebrows in Deaf culture. I'm deaf. My wife Melanie is deaf. Our son Darren is deaf. My parents are deaf. Melanie's sister Shawna is deaf. Several other relatives are deaf. Melanie and I graduated from Gallaudet University. We are familiar faces at many deaf events, local and national. We both work in deaf-related fields, she as an ASL teacher and I as a school counselor for deaf students.

So let's see, with all this beautiful deafness around me, if I can succeed at cutting myself off from the hearing world.

Let's start at my humble abode in Montgomery County, Pennsylvania. Leaving for work early in the morning, I say hello to my hearing neighbor and tell her to have a nice day. Arriving at work, I find myself working with plenty of hearing people: hearing teachers, hearing parents, and hearing workers from other agencies. By 11:00 a.m. I've interacted with about thirty hearing people, including the newspaper vendor who shoots the breeze every morning. The number will greatly increase as the day goes by.

Just for the record, I'd like to point out that my wife, my son, and I do not wear hearing aids or use any other assistive devices. It's not an act of defiance; it's a personal choice. We do have deaf friends and relatives who use hearing aids or cochlear implants, and we all agree it doesn't really matter. Each of us connects with the world in our own unique way.

My on-the-job interaction with hearing people is modest, I admit, compared to a number of deaf friends who work in other fields. Many of them work for companies where they are the only deaf employees. I consider myself lucky to work in an environment where many people sign.

Around 4:00 p.m. the workday is over. Driving home, I stop at the deli for some food. I pick up my order from the hearing deli clerk and pay the hearing cashier. After dinner with the kids, one of them has a baseball game and another has practice. I drop Brandon off at practice and watch Darren's game. I sit with the other hearing parents and briefly shoot the breeze with Darren's hearing coaches. Sometimes I pitch batting practice to Darren and Brandon's hearing teams, and other times I help the hearing coaches with pre-game field prep.

With this much involvement you'd figure I might as well coach. Been there, done that. Twice so far.

Meanwhile, Melanie drops off and picks up Lacey from softball practice. One of Lacey's hearing teammates also goes to the same weekly dance class that Lacey attends. Melanie talks with that child's hearing parents about an upcoming dance recital and makes sure that the softball and dance plans—with all those hearing people—do not conflict with each other. Afterwards, Melanie joins me at Darren's game and greets the hearing parents. Darren rips an RBI double and the hearing parents join us in giving him a round of deaf applause, waving their hands in the air.

Yes, we taught them that. See how deaf people and hearing people can get along?

At 9:00 p.m., we're back home and a few phone calls have to be made. Several hearing relatives from my mother's side of the family would like to get together soon. Calling them via videophone, we confirm dinner plans for the following week. Melanie calls her family (all hearing except for her sister) and plans are discussed for a family reunion. I'd like to note that we all have hearing relatives, and they're an important part of our lives no matter whether they sign or not.

By 10:00 p.m. the kids are in bed and Melanie and I each get a chance to surf the Internet. We check our Facebook accounts where a good portion of our friends are, you guessed it, hearing. Facebook is kind of like the great equalizer for both of us. Melanie and I will tell you that we had a closer connection to our deaf friends at Gallaudet University as compared to our hearing friends in

162

the mainstream, but on Facebook it makes no difference. Likewise on Twitter.

All right, that's enough already. You get my drift. It's simply impossible for deaf people to isolate themselves from the hearing world. Hearing relatives, friends, co-workers, classmates, neighbors, waiters and waitresses, the list goes on forever. The world is teeming with hearing people, with no shortage of them in sight. And we will always interact with them in whatever ways we can.

Active involvement in the deaf community does not in any way isolate a deaf person from the hearing world. There is no either/or, no separation. Sometimes the myth about ASL and Deaf culture isolating deaf children comes from ignorance and fear. Hearing parents who are not familiar with the deaf community may fear that they might lose their child to Deaf culture. That's a concern that can be addressed through proper education.

Sometimes it's political. Clearly there are certain people who, for whatever reason, oppose ASL. Needless to say, such people may intentionally fan the flames of the myth that ASL plus the deaf community equals isolation from society.

But a person's participation in a core group, in my opinion, is more likely to strengthen rather than isolate. If I may use my hearing neighbor as an example, she's an avid churchgoer. She faithfully attends Sunday services and participates in many of her congregation's activities. Picnics, bazaars, holiday parties, charity events, church choir, and much more. You name it, she's there. She's a better person for it.

Does this woman's church isolate her from the rest of the world? Not at all. She socializes with people from other denominations and other religions. Our neighborhood is a unique mix of people with different backgrounds and she's friendly with all of us.

Likewise, my core group is the deaf community. It strengthens me and makes me a better person. It gives me a spiritual boost, a sense of belonging. Without it I would feel empty inside. The deaf community adds a spark to my life. A spark I can share with everyone, including the hearing community.

ASL 101

As my family walked into a local McDonalds, the teenage cashier recognized right away that most of us were deaf. He caught us off-guard—and absolutely delighted us—by effortlessly switching from voice to sign language as he took our order.

I can't tell you enough what a thrill it is when hearing people start signing out of the blue.

The kid is still at it. Anytime my family and our deaf friends walk in the door, you can see the staff pull him out of the fries section or wherever he's working that day and throw him in front of the cash register.

His co-workers don't exactly back away as if to say *Watch out! Clear the perimeter or you'll catch their deaf!* Quite the opposite, they're a captive audience. They seem fascinated at how people can communicate effectively with their hands.

It's not lost on me that these are teenagers who are fascinated by sign language. I can tell you right now that if their high schools offered ASL 101, they would be among the first people to sign up. This brings me back to a point I've made many times:

MARK DROLSBAUGH

There is absolutely no excuse not to add American Sign Language as a legitimate course of instruction in schools and colleges all over the country.

And by *legitimate* I mean for credit. ASL is a widely used language that benefits countless people right here, right now. I can't tell you enough how often a group of deaf people have been surprised by store employees who knew sign language.

Some of the surprise signers are children of deaf adults (CODAs). Others happen to have a deaf friend or relative with whom they grew up and absorbed ASL by osmosis. Then there are those who tell me they took an ASL class in college. It never fails to put a smile on my face.

It's a two-way smile.

When an ASL student suddenly finds himself communicating with deaf people on the job, you can see the realization sink in.

Hey! This language actually works!

Indeed it does. It's a big thrill for an ASL student because you don't have to travel to another country to use this language. If you learn ASL, you inevitably meet people for whom it's a big part of their lives. It opens up new worlds in your own backyard.

There are numerous top-notch ASL and Deaf Studies classes at various colleges throughout the United States. This is a great thing and I hope it continues to expand.

At the high school level, however, ASL classes are few and far between. You might find an unofficial ASL Club here and there. We need more. A lot more. It would make a huge difference.

Look at it this way. High schools offer a lot of foreign languages. Spanish, French, German, Russian, Latin— whoa, waitaminute. Latin? With all due respect to the classics, what use does the average high school student have for Latin?

166

Yes, I know Latin has educational value. I'm talking about how often you use it when you talk to the Average Joe on the street.

Picture this scenario: a guy wearing a toga walks into a McDonalds and tries to order a Big Mac. He's speaking a language no one understands. The teenage kid behind the counter figures it out and asks, "You want fries with that?" in fluent Latin. Do you see this happening? Unless the Pope himself wants a Happy Meal, I don't think so.

On the other hand, how many deaf folks walk into a McDonalds (or any other restaurant, for that matter) every day? Hundreds of thousands! They ought to put *Over 2 Million Deafies Served* on the famous McDonalds logo.

And when these deafies walk into their respective restaurants, they usually get one of two responses when the waiter or cashier realizes they are deaf. Some restaurant employees are surprised but quickly recover. They say, *"Oh, I'm sorry!"* and quickly utilize pen and paper. They may also alter their speech in such a way that they're easier to lipread. Others are visibly freaked out and freeze on the spot.

"Oh, crap! He's deaf! How am I gonna talk to him?"

In either scenario, it's obvious that the employees would have a much better handle on the situation if their respective high schools and colleges had offered ASL classes. And again, no offense intended to the other languages—many of which may be practical here and there—but ASL would be used in everyday life on a regular basis.

A third—and much rarer—response is to be greeted by an employee who actually knows sign language, like the guy I described earlier. It means the world to me when this happens. I'd love it if it happened more often.

The Cochlear
Elephant in the Room

"So, what do you think about the cochlear implant?"

This is the unavoidable question at every single presentation I've ever done. If it's not addressed you'll often see a small group of hearing people—usually sign language students, inquisitive parents, or perhaps medical students interested in learning ASL—whispering amongst themselves.

"You ask him!"

"No, you ask him!"

I don't mind discussing it. If I don't, it remains the Cochlear Elephant in the Room. So go ahead and ask:

"ASL is beautiful. I get it. But why would any deaf person turn down an opportunity to hear?"

It's a delicate subject. So let's blow it right out of the water.

First, the obvious personal question: No, I don't want one. I'm happy with who I am. I did the old *go to school, get a degree, get a job, get married, buy a house, have kids, buy a minivan, raise a family* thing quite well, thank you very much. Did all of that without a cochlear implant and don't feel the need for one now.

Granted, there are other deaf people with different opinions and that's fine. There are plenty of deaf adults who have a cochlear implant. Some of them felt they had a hearing *loss* and wanted to recoup some of that loss. Others live or work in such a predominantly auditory-based environment that they felt a cochlear implant might help them keep pace. If you talk to any of these people, you will find varying degrees of satisfaction and frustration. Regardless, I respect their decision as much as I expect others to respect mine.

My opinion isn't always well-received. There's always someone who looks at me as if I'm crazy because I don't want a cochlear implant. It's hard to get my point through with those who don't understand my perspective, so that's when I break out the mind-bomb material.

Yes, I have an arsenal of mind-bombs. I like to have fun at my presentations.

"Look at it this way," I said to an audience member who thought I was one sandwich short of a picnic. "I have a beautiful daughter. I know that when she grows up, she's inevitably going to face her share of harassment and discrimination. It's a known fact that in the corporate world, women get paid seventy-five percent of what men make even though they're doing the same job. But I have faith in my daughter. She's resilient. She's going to make it in this male-dominated society. Do you see me running to the doctor to inquire about a penis implant?"

The silence in the room is deafening after that one.

Then there was the time I went on a diatribe about the National Institute on Deafness and Other Communication Disorders. I took offense at how they lumped *Deafness* with *Other Communication Disorders*. Here's my response to that:

169

If you introduce me to someone and I promptly start barking like a dog, then you could make an argument that I have a communication disorder. If I greet people by sniffing their armpits or insist on perpetually ordering my Happy Meal in Klingon, then likewise you'd have a good case. Obviously I don't do any of that, so I don't understand why my family and closest friends have to deal with this offensive label.

But if "National Institute on Deafness and Other Communication Disorders" is acceptable, then I say it's time we jump on the bandwagon and expand on this for the betterment of society. How about if for good measure we set up the following organizations:

National Institute on Racial Diversity and Other Pigment Disorders

National Institute on Women and Other Penis Disorders

National Institute on Religion and Other Delusional Disorders

National Institute on Politics and Other Pathological Lying Disorders

Have I offended anyone? Good! That's how I feel when I see "and Other Communication Disorders" attached to the community where I belong.

Need I go on? Hell yes, I will. I'm having too much fun with this.

I'm deaf as a post. If you're reading this, we're connecting somehow. I made a point, and you got it. Doesn't matter if you agree or disagree. Because, gosh darn it, we communicated! Congratulations.

My ability to communicate isn't limited to my writing. If you want to get technical you could add e-mail, text messages, videophone, and whatnot. But I want to emphasize that I do pretty well in person, too. Ditto for my family, several of whom are deaf. We communicate just fine with each other. In two languages. I also know other deaf people who are fluent in as many as four languages. And we all bend over backwards to communicate with people who do not know sign language. However we work it out, it's all good.

All right, that's enough of that. Back to cochlear implants. We've established that I don't want one, and at the same time we should respect the decisions of those who do. Which brings us to the biggest can of worms: Implanting deaf babies and children who are too young to make an informed decision of their own.

First, let's address the language issue. I—and many deaf advocates—have argued that early exposure to language is critical. ASL is clearly the best head start for language acquisition that you can give to a baby (any baby, deaf or hearing). A baby starts gesturing and signing long before he or she is able to utilize his or her vocal cords. No matter if deaf or hearing, you can wire a baby's mind for language long before he or she speaks. This has proven to be a significant advantage in language acquisition.

However, if you advocate on behalf of early language acquisition via ASL, the Auditory-Verbal Therapy (AVT) camp will respond by saying the same argument applies to the cochlear implant. A young child's mind is like a sponge—so if you have a deaf child implanted as early as possible, this also improves exposure to sound and language during the critical window for optimal speech/language acquisition. (Both the ASL and AVT camp agree that if language acquisition hasn't sufficiently developed by age five, a child will most likely have a language delay for life.)

I'm going to go off on a tangent right here and say I do not fault parents for implanting their children. They want to do everything they can to provide the best opportunities for their kids. My concern is that ASL often

171

gets swept under the rug and many families miss out. Families who do not want cochlear implants for their deaf children are often not told that ASL is an option. Families who went ahead with the cochlear implant are either not told about ASL or told to avoid it. This is a travesty because ASL can easily fill in the gaps for many children with cochlear implants who are still struggling to acquire language. On several occasions while working with deaf children who have cochlear implants, parents have told me "the doctors never said anything about this (ASL). I wish they told us before." Look, I know cochlear implants are here to stay. It's the either/or mentality that I wish would go away.

My opinion about the cochlear implant has never been set in stone. It has evolved over time because it is no longer *out there.* I hated it when it first came out because it represented yet another attempt to trample over the progress made in deaf education. ASL was thrown under the bus after the Milan Conference of 1880 and that knocked everything out of whack for *decades.* Generations of deaf children were denied communication access in the classroom

ASL eventually made a comeback in the 1970s. Once again, there was one hundred percent access in the classroom for deaf students. Then along came the cochlear implant and *whoomp,* the rug got pulled out from under ASL again. Of course, most hearing parents relate to the concept of helping their children improve their hearing ability more than they can relate to the concept of a Deaf culture. As a result, the cochlear implant had a lot of people jumping off the ASL bandwagon. I resented that.

As much as I was able to resent the ideal that the cochlear implant represents, I cannot resent actual human beings. So whereas in the mid 1990's the cochlear implant was *out there,* today I am surrounded by people who have one. I cherish each and every one of them and cannot let political ideals cloud our relationship.

So who are these people and how well are they doing with their cochlear implants? And how has this affected my opinion of it? Quite frankly, it looks like a Bell Curve to me. I will leave the door open that my opinion may be biased, for reasons I will explain soon.

Of the deaf adults and children I know who have a cochlear implant, a small percentage absolutely love it. Based on feedback I've heard from others, this small percentage seems to be growing over time as technology improves. They report being able to use the phone and being able to converse with hearing relatives or co-workers they could not understand before. Some of them are doing so well that I wondered if this book would soon be obsolete ("No need to advocate on behalf of deaf issues anymore—there aren't any deaf people left!"). Most of these people, however, still report having difficulty in large groups. In a nutshell, you could say this group experienced a significant improvement in hearing ability where they went from "profoundly deaf" to "hard of hearing."

Conversely, a small percentage of the people I know with cochlear implants absolutely hate it. Some of them had medical complications and for others, it just didn't work well enough. They no longer use their cochlear implants and often tell others it's not worth the hassle.

A great majority of the implanted people I know are somewhere in between on the continuum. Ask them and they'll say something to the effect of "I like it," "It's all right," or "It has its pros and cons." Of this larger majority, half of them regularly wear their implants and the others are noncommittal.

As for my possible bias, I have to point out that of all the deaf people I know who have a cochlear implant, each one of them is a member of the deaf community.

Regardless of how well (or not well) they're doing with their implants, they're still deaf. They always have and still use ASL to communicate with their deaf peers and feel most comfortable within the deaf community. I've often thought to myself—especially when working with implanted children in deaf schools—*if the cochlear implant is so good, why are CI users still here?*

And there's the rub. I don't know any of the implanted deaf children or adults *out there* in the mainstream. I don't know how well (or not well) they're doing. My opinions are pretty much based on interaction with implanted individuals who are involved with the deaf community.

So when my son Darren—who has had an ASL interpreter all through elementary and middle school—expressed how bored he was at being the only deaf kid in his school, I called the school district to ask if it would be possible to get all of the deaf and hard of hearing children together for a social gathering. Their response:

All of the other deaf kids in the district have cochlear implants and don't use sign language. They're doing fine so there's not really much of a need to do anything.

Ugh. I wondered what the school district meant by *doing fine*. So did my wife, Melanie, who took it one step further and asked the district—which historically has made its PSSA (Pennsylvania System of School Assessment) scores known to the public—if they could show how deaf and hard of hearing students have performed in various subject areas. Surprisingly, there was no data for that.

This troubled me and I continued to wonder about all of those kids who are *doing fine*. For instance, if you ask any of Darren's teachers how he's doing, they'll tell you he's *doing fine* because he's on the honor roll and has scored "advanced" all across the board in his most recent PSSAs. But what they can't tell you about is the isolation

174

he feels as the only deaf student in his school—they rarely see it, and he doesn't volunteer this information for them. He has brought it up at home, however, so we know he's not entirely *doing fine* and we're looking into making some changes that will result in a more enjoyable academic experience.

So again, what about all of those mainstreamed cochlear implant students who are *doing fine?* Most of the information I have is hearsay—it's adults speaking out on behalf of the children. I usually get the standard *doing fine* from teachers and parents when I ask around.

Yes, we need to make sure we interview the kids. I'll never forget that Family Learning Vacation in Maine where most of the parents said their kids were doing fine, but in a separate workshop the kids themselves said otherwise. Kids need more opportunities to say what's on their minds.

Not everyone gives me a *doing fine.* Some parents have made comments along the lines of "he's doing fine, but it's a lot of work" and "she's pretty much functioning like a hard of hearing child." Others have marveled at how well the cochlear implant helps their children in the classroom, but "socially, he doesn't have that many friends."

While I was wondering about kids with cochlear implants in the mainstream, a friend referred me to *Cochlear Implant Online*, a website that shares inspirational cochlear implant stories. I found a blog post covering the 2011 Northeast Cochlear Implant Conference, which included a *We Hear You, Now Hear Us* panel of middle school and high students with cochlear implants.

As I read their comments, it validated my belief that we need to allow students more opportunities to speak up. The students on the panel indicated that they needed additional services in the classroom (notetakers, CART, C-Print, and preferential seating), and they also said that they often missed out on what was said during sports, sleepovers, and movies (they made it clear that they prefer to rent movies with captions).

Furthermore, there's a great article by Karen Putz titled *Calling Our Bluff: Using Communication Strategies in Social Situations.* A couple of chapters ago, you'll recall me using social bluffing techniques at an outdoor party; in Karen's article, you'll find two deaf adults with cochlear implants (one of them bilaterally implanted) who also admit to social bluffing. One of them says it's tiring to keep up in conversations with hearing people, and the other offers a list of alternate strategies that are much better than bluffing.

Which brings me back to my point: No matter how successful a person is with a cochlear implant, each cochlear implant user has his or her share of issues to deal with. And the only person who truly understands the issues that come with a cochlear implant is another person with a cochlear implant. So as much as I wouldn't want to see a deaf student isolated in the mainstream, I wouldn't want a cochlear implant user isolated either. Not only would I want cochlear implant users to have frequent opportunities to interact with each other, but also with other deaf children who may or may not use assistive devices.

For whatever reason, there are people who don't want kids with cochlear implants to be exposed to other deaf people, especially deaf people who sign. This is a crock. During the Sertoma Fantasy Baseball Camp (Harrisburg, PA) in the summer of 2009, I personally witnessed kids with cochlear implants interacting with signing deaf kids. Everyone got along great.

Socialization is hard enough for deaf and hard of hearing kids of all backgrounds. Why would anyone want to limit who they can interact with? It's ridiculous. In the words of the late, great, infamous Rodney King: *Can't we all get along?*

Another thing that gets to me is how many of these mainstreamed students with cochlear implants wind up going to Gallaudet University or the National Technical Institute for the Deaf. Regardless of how well they did with their implants, they still feel the need to go somewhere where they can identify with their peers. Why do they have to wait until college to get this opportunity?

Bottom line: Deaf, hard of hearing, oral, signing, cochlear implanted... it doesn't matter. Everyone needs a place to belong.

But What About the
Hard of Hearing?

Count them in. The hard of hearing population is *huge*. They significantly outnumber the deaf. And yet this significantly large hard of hearing population is often overlooked.

The deaf community is relatively small but its cultural impact is phenomenal. Do a Google search on "Deaf" or "ASL" and you'll find a plethora of websites, blogs, and general information on what it means to be deaf. You'll find community events, artists, entertainers, poets, Deaf Studies curriculums, and much more. Fun, fun, fun!

As for the hard of hearing? I Googled "hard of hearing" and had to sift through websites that focused mostly on rehabilitation, advocacy, assistive devices, strategies for communicating with the hearing world, and a mostly pathological approach towards hearing loss. One website even featured a picture of a doctor peering into someone's ear.

Nice, but can we forget about the ears for a moment and focus on what it means to be hard of hearing? More specifically, what does it feel like? What are the attitudes, feelings, and experiences that are unique to the hard of hearing?

All of the aforementioned rehabilitation stuff is well-intentioned and in fact helpful in many aspects. At the same time, a caveat: Sometimes it may actually reinforce a negative mindset.

Many hard of hearing people, for one reason or the other, have this internalized belief that it is entirely their responsibility to communicate effectively with the hearing world at large. They'll blame themselves if they fail. That's a shame because there's nothing to apologize for.

During my elementary and middle school years, I was hard of hearing. I remember it as something very different than being deaf. Back in those days, it did indeed seem like the burden of communication was placed entirely on my shoulders. If I got frustrated, the response would be along the lines of *you should sit up front, you should wear your hearing aid, you should pay attention* and other maddening *you shoulds*.

After I went completely deaf, things changed for the better. No longer was I stuck on the fence in a netherworld where I was not quite hearing and not quite deaf. I was deaf. Period. Sign language became my preferred mode of communication. People noticed. I was accepted as a deaf person. The appropriate accommodations were provided whenever needed. Nice, but where was all of this understanding before, when it was needed most?

Obviously, most hard of hearing people have significantly more residual hearing and speech ability than the deaf. This can actually be more of a curse than a blessing. Whereas mainstream society at large is more sensitive to the needs of the culturally Deaf, it tends to take the hard of hearing population for granted.

A deaf person is more visibly deaf in that he or she uses ASL. But for the hard of hearing, oftentimes hearing people assume, *Oh, he speaks so well, he's doing fine* without stopping to think that good speech or not, the hard of hearing person has to put in considerable effort. Many people forget that communication is a two way street; just because a hard of hearing person speaks clearly does not in any way guarantee that he or she *hears* clearly.

Although there are organizations that advocate on behalf of the hard of hearing—the Hearing Loss Association of America, for one—there's no bona fide hard of hearing culture. Here's a close (and sometimes tongue-in-cheek) look at why this is so:

- There's no HHSL, or Hard of Hearing Sign Language. Therefore the hard of hearing aren't as visible. There are many hard of hearing people you wouldn't even know are hard of hearing unless they personally told you.

- There's never been a *Hard of Hearing President Now* protest at Gallaudet University.

- Some hard of hearing people blend in so well— or appear to blend in so well—with mainstream society that few people take them seriously when they ask for support or assistance.

- There are numerous ASL and Deaf Studies classes nationwide but Hard of Hearing Studies classes are nowhere to be found. (Pathological studies of hearing loss don't count. I'm talking about a state of *being*, not a medical profile of the inner ear.)

- The hard of hearing population is remarkably diverse. Degree of hearing loss, age of onset, communication preferences, the use of assistive devices, knowledge of sign language, interaction with other deaf and hard of hearing people, and

180

personal philosophy of what it means to be deaf or hard of hearing are all factors that greatly vary. (You could argue that the same factors exist in the Deaf world, but the Deaf world has a common thread—ASL and Deaf culture—that connects everyone).

It needs to be emphasized that any group—deaf, culturally Deaf, late-deafened, or the hard of hearing—deserves recognition and respect for who they are.

For this reason I ask school districts and politicians to be as sensitive to the needs of the hard of hearing as much as the needs of the deaf. The same goes for people with cochlear implants, many of whom are in fact functionally hard of hearing.

It pains me to know that there are hard of hearing children who are alone in the mainstream. They, too, deserve the quality of interaction that comes from being in the company of their true peers. I've actually inquired about them a few times and have been told they're doing fine.

Perhaps the best way to wrap this up is to include a story from someone who has been there, done that. Michelle Corallo, a colleague I mentioned a few chapters ago, was gracious enough to submit a riveting account of her hard of hearing experience. Here's her story:

One day, about 40 years ago, a little girl was playing on the beach with a friend. They were digging a giant hole near the ocean and every once in a while they would giggle with delight as waves would spill into their hole. The little girl then looked up from her digging efforts to make a comment to her friend when she saw that she was gone. She quickly sat up and looked around the beach. She spotted her friend and several other children running to the top of the beach where an ice cream man was shaking something in the air. The little girl scratched her head and wondered to herself, "How do they always figure out when the ice cream man is here?"

The next month this little girl started kindergarten. About three months into school, she and all of her classmates lined up to pay a visit to the nurse. They took turns putting funny-looking things on their heads. Each child would sit down, put these funny things on their heads and then raised one hand and then the other. The little girl thought it was fascinating and could not wait for her turn. And although the little girl could not tell time, she noticed on the analog clock that the skinniest of the lines would go about half way around the circle before the nurse said, "You are done. Next!" This seemed to be the pattern for all of the children and then it was the little girl's turn. The little girl sat down and the nurse put the funny thing on her head (it pulled her hair, she remembered). The nurse said, "When you hear a sound, raise your hand. If it's in this one (pointing to the left ear), raise this hand. If it's this one (pointing to the right ear), raise this one."

So, the little girl, always wanting to be compliant, sat and waited.... and waited ....and waited. From time to time she raised her hand and as she looked up she saw a puzzled look on the nurses' face. More unusual, though, was that skinniest of arms on the clock. It went around... and around... and around......

When the testing was done, the nurse told the little girl to sit and wait as the other children had their turns. The nurse then took the girl and led her to her teacher. Looking up at the nurse as she spoke to the teacher, she watched her say, "She's not retarded. She just can't hear."

That little girl was me. The year was 1971, four years before the infamous Public Law 94-142 (Education of All Handicapped Children Act, now known as IDEA) was passed. According to this new enactment, states had to develop and implement policies that assured a free appropriate public education to all children with disabilities.

At the time my hearing loss was detected, the school provided me with speech lessons. Twice a week I went to speech lessons to have lemon paste put on the roof on my mouth so I could learn the proper placement of my tongue to help me remember how to make the "t" sound. I must have really benefitted from those services since most times, when I meet someone new and I tell them about my deafness, they will say something to the effect of, "Wow, your speech is really good." In the back of my head I always want to say, "Oh yeah? Ask me what I learned in school."

For sixteen years, I virtually sat at a desk at elementary school, junior high school, high school and college and learned nothing. And for sixteen years, I somehow advanced through each grade. I can tell you how I did it, and I'm not proud. I copied, plagiarized, wrote answers on my hands, had test stolen for me so I could memorize the answers, and passed. It was the only way I knew how to get by and for lack of a better word, it worked. I was in the lowest classes all through school and out of my high school class of 425 students, I graduated number 418. But hey, my speech was good, so what's the big deal?

I applied to college because I was hanging out with really smart, funny, and cool girls who were all moving on to further their educations. I wanted to be just like them. I applied to a few schools and with my mom went to visit one specific program (where they specialized in Deaf Education) for a tour and interview.

As we sat down, the administrator asked a few questions and looked through my application. And then...

"I notice you have a speech impediment," she said. "Where is that from?"

"Well, I guess it would be from my hearing loss," I replied.

"Why isn't this marked on your application in the disabilities area?"

"Well," I stammered. "I never really considered myself disabled... are you saying I should have marked it?"

The administrator sighed.

"With your poor SAT scores, class rank and grades, I don't know of any program that is going to accept you."

At that point I stood up and motioned for my mother to leave with me.

"I'm not going to be forced to check a box so I can get accepted into a program," I said to no one in particular. "Either they want me or they don't. I guess I'm going the local community college."

A few schools did accept me. I went to a state school near my home before transferring to a small school down south where they had a teacher of the deaf program. Needless to say, college was just as frustrating for me and I got by the only way I could and continued to obtain my very poor grade point average of 1.60.

A funny thing happened at my school. They had a great interpreter program there for deaf and hard of hearing students. I was provided with an interpreter in each of my classes, sat in the front so I could have full access, and also had a note-taker so I could attend to the interpreter. There was a small problem though...I couldn't sign! So there I was, once again, not following anything that was being taught in school. But hey, the speech thing? I was the champ.

Once I finished college, I became a teacher aide in a class with students who were deaf and hard of hearing. Two things happened that year. I started learning sign language, and the teacher expected me to teach lessons from time to time. I would prepare for the lessons by reading the curriculum, trying to really understand what I needed to teach, and all of a sudden I was keenly aware that I did not have a foundation of knowledge. So from that point on I decided to learn the most basic of things I did not obtain in school. On the one hand, I learned new things. On the other hand, my self-esteem—which wasn't that great to begin with—took another hit when I realized how much I didn't know. It was damaging to my belief in myself: After all these years, how could I not know so much?

I taught for another year before moving to Geneva, Switzerland and worked with a family who had a daughter who was deaf and blind. Afterward, I came back to the States and taught again for another three years. As much as I loved teaching, the deaf and hard of hearing children were transferred out of the school where I worked and were mainstreamed into their local school district programs. I realized I really wanted to work with these students, but in a different capacity.

I looked into the School Psychology program at Gallaudet University and was very intrigued by what they offered. I sent in an application and then went to Washington DC to interview with the director of the program. After we spoke for a while, she took a deep breath.

"Your GRE scores are terrible. Your college transcript shows a very low GPA and you graduated at the bottom *of your class. Tell me... why we should accept you into our program?"*

"I need to be given one chance to prove to myself that I can do this," I replied. "I'm getting married in a few months and plan on having children in the future. I cannot have children without knowing that I'm capable of learning and that I'm not a stupid person. It wouldn't be fair for them to have a mother who thinks so poorly of herself. If you can give me just one chance... one semester... to prove that I can do well in school without plagiarizing, copying, or stealing tests... that would mean so much to me in so many different ways."

The director sat quietly for a few moments.

"Okay. You get one semester to show what you can do. Anything lower than a 3.00 in your grades and you're out. Are we clear?"

I stated that I understood. I left her office scared to death of what I was going to be confronted with, but I was ready for the challenge.

My classes had no more than seven students in them. The teachers signed and talked at the same time. I had peers who took notes for those of us who were deaf and hard of hearing. It was clearly the least restrictive educational environment that I had been entitled to in my whole life. The program was very challenging, and I can honestly say that I never worked so hard in my life for anything. Because of this program and the support services that were provided to me, I was able to graduate magna cum laude from Gallaudet, earning a master's degree and a specialist's degree with a cumulative 3.98 grade point average.

I'm a mother now. I share my story with my children often to remind them that we are all given obstacles. And obstacles are to be seen as stepping stones to success and opportunities, regardless of how long it takes you to get there. While sometimes I wonder how my life would have turned out if I had been in an educational environment with the appropriate services from the very beginning, at the same time I know I wouldn't have wound up being the child advocate that I am today. I wouldn't have it any other way.

A Truth for All Ages

While surfing the Internet, I came across some studies that said people who have a strong circle of friends tend to live longer. This inspired me to pose the following question on my *DrolzUncensored* Twitter account:

Research has shown that social life is correlated with longevity. So should we assume mainstreaming is hazardous to our health?

It's a valid question. As the stories in this book have shown, being the only deaf student in your school can be stressful. A case can be made that deaf peers and role models are essential for our physical and emotional health.

It turns out that this is a truth for all ages.

I wrote about this in *Deaf Again*. Several years ago my paternal grandparents, Michael and Marjorie "Nana" Novak, both deaf, had a wonderful experience at a deaf assisted-living facility that was known as the Nevil Home. Here's the excerpt:

The phone rang, and it was a relative calling to inform us that Nana had suffered a nasty stroke. She would never be the same again. Visiting her in the hospital, my family and I discovered that she was unable to walk, unable to use her right hand, unable to read, and was confusing various relatives' names. She referred to my dad as "Robert" and Uncle Bob as "Charlie." She was in for a long period of rehabilitation.

Slowly, Nana began to make enough progress so that she could be discharged from the hospital. But before returning home, she would have to spend some time in a rehabilitation center. This turned out to be Hopkins House in Jenkintown. It was a fine facility and they did everything they could to help Nana recover. She slowly regained her ability to walk, although she would still need to spend much time in a wheelchair.

Everything else, however, came along slowly. Her right hand was still curled up, unable to function normally. She complained that she could no longer read books or follow the captions on television. Interestingly, her signing skills remained intact, although she was limited to signing with one hand.

Shortly after returning home, Nana had yet another setback. She collapsed from a second stroke and Mike was barely able to assist her in time to save her life. After another hospital stay, it was determined that Nana needed to live in a place where she could have round-the-clock supervision. Grudgingly, she and Mike accepted the family's strong recommendation that they move to the Nevil Home, a nursing home for the deaf in Media, Pennsylvania.

Of course, no couple likes to leave the freedom of their own place to live in a nursing home. Nana might have lost some function, but her wits were still intact:

"Put me out to pasture, eh? Why not take me behind the barn and shoot me?"

Soon, however, Nana and Mike were settled down at the Nevil Home and having a great time. There were nightly events featuring movies, games, and occasional *trips such as an excursion to Atlantic City. The other residents were deaf and most of the staff signed, so Nana and Mike were actually socializing a whole lot more than they ever had at their old apartment complex.*

Gradually, Nana regained that old spark we hadn't seen for a long time. She hurled friendly insults at Mike and even threw the Kleenex box at him whenever he dozed off in front of the TV. She cracked one-liners like Sophia on The Golden Girls. *She jokingly complained that Mike had a roving eye for the other ladies ("Eighty years old and he thinks he's a swinger!"). Mike would play along mischievously and flirt with female residents who walked by. The smiles on their faces said it all. The Nana I knew was back.*

It turned into one big party. It even reached the point where our family smuggled in beer and whiskey for Mike. It wasn't permitted, but so what. If these were the twilight years, why shouldn't they enjoy every minute of it?

Although Nana would never be exactly the same as she was before the strokes, the progress she made at the Nevil Home was amazing. I couldn't help but notice the difference: At Hopkins House she was surrounded by the most professional, competent staff of physical therapists you could ever ask for, yet her heart wasn't really in it. She made enough progress to go home, but just barely. At the Nevil Home, Nana clearly enjoyed life again and practically turned into a party animal. Her spirits rose high enough that she was able to bounce back considerably from her strokes. I really believe that having deaf friends, family, and an ASL-competent staff around her is what gave Nana the emotional boost that allowed her to regain much of what she had lost.

It wasn't long before she was once again able to read and do her favorite crossword puzzles. Yes, she still had to spend time in a wheelchair and she also struggled with her short-term memory. Nonetheless, she had come a long way. It was a remarkable comeback. The bottom line was that she was once again enjoying a quality of life she hadn't had since her days as the cook at a local deaf club.

If you stop and think about it, you'll notice a parallel here. Deaf advocates have often argued that deaf children deserve the quality of life that is available to them when you allow them to interact with their deaf peers. In this case, with Nana and Mike, I had discovered that it was a universal truth that applied to all ages. The Nevil Home allowed them to rediscover that missing spark, a spark that gave them strength to recover physically, emotionally, and spiritually.

Nana and Mike would spend the next seven years at the Nevil Home, where our family would get together to celebrate Christmas and other joyous occasions on a regular basis. When they eventually passed away— within months of each other (Nana in the Fall of 1991 and Mike in the Spring of 1992)—we were grateful for all of the wonderful memories.

From Madness to
Common Sense

All you really need to address the problems in the mainstream is a healthy dose of common sense. There are plenty of simple solutions that could improve deaf education on so many levels.

The best way to start is to simply ask for and value the opinion of the deaf community. You'd be surprised at how many schools, agencies, and organizations serving the deaf are run by hearing people who never bothered to consult with actual deaf people. The National Association of the Deaf (NAD) knows this. It's no coincidence that the motto of the 2012 NAD conference was *Nothing About Us, Without Us.* Deaf people need to have a say in the education of deaf children. Who better to ask than those who have been there, done that?

Hospitals and Early Intervention programs need to include deaf professionals when they advise parents of deaf children. It's unfortunate how grieving parents of newly-identified deaf babies have often been told to avoid sign language and the deaf community. Countless deaf children grow up in isolation as a result of this misguided advice. This could easily be avoided by making sure there

192

are deaf mentors available to consult with parents from the very beginning.

More advocacy, parent education, and political support are also needed to reverse the trend of deaf schools being treated as dumping grounds. A deaf school should be considered as a healthy primary option, not a last-ditch attempt after all other options have failed.

Granted, demographics don't always make a deaf school feasible. You obviously can't run a deaf school if there aren't enough deaf children in your region. I understand this, but I implore school districts to please do everything they can to reduce the number of solitary deaf children—also known as *onestreamed* kids and *solitaires*—in their respective educational settings. As often as possible, allow deaf mainstreamed students to attend the same schools and to have the opportunity to interact in afterschool programs.

Another possibility: If there aren't enough deaf kids in a particular region to be able to operate a deaf school, open the door for a *signing school* by including deaf children, siblings of deaf children, children of deaf adults, and anyone in the community who would like their education offered in sign language. My inspiration for this comes from the Pennsylvania School for the Deaf's Community Classroom. Many hearing children, including two of mine, have attended this program. It's offered to hearing children between the ages of 3-5 and they get a complete preschool education in ASL. I can tell you firsthand that an early education in ASL gives these kids a significant head start for their grade school years.

Yes, I'm aware that there are some people who aren't thrilled with the idea of deaf and hearing kids learning together in a signing environment. There are concerns that too many hearing people in what's supposed to be a predominantly deaf environment can marginalize the deaf experience.

Shortly before this book went to print, the television series *Switched at Birth* addressed the same issue. During a *Take Back Carlton* student protest, deaf high school students demanded that their school be kept open (it was supposed to be closed due to budget cuts) and that hearing students be kept out. This was just a fictional television show, but it was based on real-life events and it elicited very real emotional responses within the deaf community.

I understand the desire to keep traditional deaf residential schools intact just the way they are. This would be my first choice, too. But if demographics and economics prevent this, I'm fine with a signing deaf/hearing school as Plan B. I would much rather be in a signing school with a mix of deaf and hearing students than be stuck alone as the only deaf student in an all-hearing school.

Besides, deaf college students have the option of attending Gallaudet University—with its predominantly deaf student body—or the National Technical Institute for the Deaf, which is one of eight colleges on the predominantly hearing campus of the Rochester Institute of Technology. It comes down to personal preference. If deaf college students can choose between such programs, then deaf high school students should have the same opportunity.

All right, back to reality. Mainstream programs are still the first option for most deaf children. Obviously, mainstreaming can be a stressful experience. For this reason I believe there should be a standard introductory workshop for parents and teachers of mainstreamed deaf children. Something along the lines of *Mainstreaming 101: What Your Deaf Kid Isn't Telling You*. I would offer my son Darren as Exhibit A. Could you imagine what this workshop would look like? How about this:

The lights dim, and a PowerPoint presentation begins.

"Okay, everyone, here's a copy of Darren's report card. Nice, huh?"

Polite applause.

"Here's a video of him on the baseball team. Look at him smash that pitch for a double."

More applause.

"Here's another video of him making a diving catch at second base."

Oohs and aahs.

"Back to school. Give him a hand for his science project. Look at that volcano. He sure nailed it, huh?"

An even louder round of applause for the kid kicking ass in the mainstream.

"Okay, thank you. That's enough of that. Let's switch things up a bit. Here's a picture of Darren riding on the school bus. See the expression on his face?"

The room goes silent.

"Here he is sitting in the cafeteria. Do you have any idea what the other kids are talking about? Neither does he."

Crickets chirping.

"Back to baseball. Here's Darren sitting on the bench in between innings. You see him talking to anyone? Me neither."

At this point, I would offer some advice to fill in the gaps. Among the ways to do that:

- Ask the school district for regularly scheduled social events with other mainstreamed deaf students. (Some programs are already doing this. The Rochester School for the Deaf, for example, has a program where mainstreamed students gather there for study hall and social time after school.)

- Seek out the deaf community and attend their events.

- Find successful deaf role models with varying backgrounds and allow deaf children to interact with them. There's a continuum of deaf people with different communication styles, and it's healthy for deaf children to see this. It allows them to see that there are many ways they can succeed in this world.

- End the practice of separating deaf children who communicate differently. Signing, speaking, and use of technological devices do not have to be mutually exclusive. Again, deaf children need to see the diversity amongst each other. To shield a deaf child from other deaf people who are different from them is to impose limits. It blocks deaf children from realizing their potential.

- Ask mainstream schools to offer American Sign Language classes as part of their curriculum. It's a legitimate language. (Wouldn't it be great if those hearing kids in the cafeteria could sign with your deaf child?)

- Look for and send your child to a deaf summer camp. It's worth it.

Advocacy at schools, local hospitals, and Early Intervention programs are just the tip of the iceberg. We need a global approach. Most people in the world at large know very little about what it means to be deaf. In order to open more minds, deaf people need to be more visible on television and in movies. The deaf cast members of the aforementioned television series *Switched at Birth* is a fantastic example. Not only is deaf actor Sean

Berdy immensely popular with deaf teens, but he has tremendous crossover appeal in the mainstream. Thanks to Sean, there are hearing kids all over the country saying *hey, that deaf guy is pretty cool*. They don't feel sorry for Sean because he's deaf. They actually look up to him and are more apt to enroll in an ASL class.

Getting back to the subject of ASL classes, we need more of them. We need them in schools, colleges, summer programs, and even in the workplace (such as ASL training that is offered to police, firemen, and emergency medical personnel). ASL classes are crucial in spreading deaf awareness on a level you just don't get anywhere else. Most (if not all) of ASL instructors insist on doing a lot more than just teach sign language. They require their students to read deaf literature, attend shows featuring deaf performing artists, and interact with members of the deaf community.

Another thing about ASL classes: If an ASL curriculum was added to schools all over the country, it would greatly reduce the need to advocate on behalf of deaf awareness to doctors, politicians, school districts, and so on. The next generation of professionals would already have a solid foundation of deaf awareness by the time they finish high school.

Everything I've said so far is probably not going to be well-received by organizations that prefer to focus solely on listening and speaking. Yes, I'm talking about the oralists.

I'm not going to exclude oral schools and organizations. I have a suggestion for them, too. I think oral schools should offer ASL lessons. Seriously, why not? I have no problem with whatever communication methodology a deaf person prefers. I don't care if a deaf person would rather speak or sign. Whatever works for each individual is fine. It's the One Size Fits All approach that concerns me. Where there's One Size Fits All, there will be people who fall through the cracks.

It is for this reason you'll see ASL-friendly deaf schools offering a plethora of options that match each student. In addition to accessible signing staff, you'll find speech teachers, audiologists, cochlear implant support, and more. You'll find classes taught in ASL. You'll find classes with spoken English support. It's all there. Deaf schools go out of their way to accommodate everyone.

Note: It's been brought to my attention that "options" is a misleading word. "Options" can give the false impression to parents of deaf children that they're supposed to choose between this and that. It doesn't have to be that way. A better word, I've been told, is "opportunity." You can have the opportunity to use a hearing aid, your speech skills, and your signing skills. You don't have to pick one over the other. Take the opportunity to use any combination that benefits you.

Now I have to ask: The same way a deaf school provides opportunities to enhance your speech, why shouldn't an oral school provide opportunities to enhance your ASL? If a predominantly signing deaf child gets speech therapy twice a week, it only makes sense that a predominantly speaking deaf child should get ASL therapy twice a week. Besides, emerging research has shown that sign vocabulary can enhance spoken vocabulary for those who have speech skills. There is simply no excuse to separate the two. Balance it out and make sure no one falls through the cracks.

I know so many former oral school students who eventually went on to Gallaudet University or the National Technical Institute for the Deaf. They all sign now, but many of them had to attend sessions such as Gallaudet's New Signers Program to help them get acclimated. I'm sure twice-weekly ASL therapy at their old schools would have gone a long way towards making this transition easier. It's kind of sad they had to wait so long to find what worked best for them.

Time and time again I've met deaf people who describe themselves as former oralists. The irony doesn't escape me that I've never seen someone describe himself as a former signer.

Deaf schools are on to something, folks. They know a thing or two about language accessibility. They've created an environment where deaf children of all backgrounds can thrive. And yet, maddeningly, there's still a huge push to shut them down.

End the madness. Keep the deaf schools and deaf programs open. They do more for the wellbeing of deaf children than anyone in mainstream society could ever imagine.

Epilogue

"Darren," I sighed. "I know you're fed up with mainstreaming. Unfortunately, you can't go to RSD. I told you this before. You have to live in New York to go to RSD."

"Aw, crap," Darren replied. "Some of my good friends from camp go there."

"I know. It sucks that you can't join them. But how about MSSD? It's a federally-funded program. You can live anywhere in the United States and be eligible for MSSD."

"Yeah. I know a few people there and they like it very much."

"Awesome. MSSD looks like a good match, but I'd like you to finish middle school first."

"Sure," Darren shrugged. "That makes sense."

"Our school district is a little weird. Middle school is grades seven, eight, and nine. North Penn High School is only for grades ten, eleven, and twelve. Most high schools are for grades nine through twelve, so you might think North Penn is smaller. It's not. It has three thousand students. I don't want you being the only deaf kid there."

"That's good to know."

"I'm not that stupid," I continued. "But you did really well in the eighth grade so you might as well finish ninth.

Then you're out of here. You can go to MSSD for your sophomore year. Fair enough?"

"Fair enough."

This was just one of several ongoing conversations about leaving the mainstream for a deaf school. The question was no longer *if*, but *when*. For as much as I understood the value of a good deaf program, I wrestled with the timing of switching schools.

The North Penn School District is one of the best in Pennsylvania. Darren's teachers at both his elementary school and middle school had succeeded in giving him a fantastic education. If ninth grade was technically an extra year of middle school, I figured, he might as well grab it. Besides, Darren seemed a bit too young to be sent three hours away to the Model Secondary School for the Deaf.

Yes, I selfishly wanted to keep him around for one more year. This isn't easy.

"Okay, Darren," I added. "I'm pretty sure you want to go back to Camp Mark Seven. Correct?"

"Definitely," Darren replied.

"Great. I'm thinking you can grit it out in the mainstream for one more year if you balance out the frustrating stuff with baseball, CM7, and staying in touch with your CM7 friends year-round."

"I've got them all on Facebook," he grinned.

"All right. We're good. Our decision is final."

Or was it?

Later that summer—the summer of 2013—Darren eagerly returned to Camp Mark Seven. But it was not the same program he'd gone to in years past. This time, Camp Mark Seven hosted their first annual Deaf Film Camp. In addition to the usual fun outdoor activities, campers got to work closely with some of the most talented deaf professionals in cinematography and animation. Among the artists Darren collaborated with were Wayne Betts Jr.

and Braam Jordaan. As Wayne and Braam began sharing their expertise, the realization suddenly struck Darren:

So this is what a deaf classroom feels like.

Two weeks later, I joined the campers for movie night. The staff had rented out a movie theater in Old Forge and played all of the videos that the kids had worked on. As expected, it was very inspiring. And the best was yet to come.

At the end of the show, they played a music video featuring renowned ASL performer Azora Telford. The song was OneRepublic's *Feel Again* and the lyrics had a powerful connection to anyone who found the Deaf world after years of being mainstreamed. One of the lines in the song hit me like an anvil.

I was a lonely soul but that's the old me...

I shifted in my seat and took a deep breath. Wayne, Braam, and the rest of their crew (including the kids who starred in and assisted with the production of the video) had taken this song to a whole new level. From a Deaf perspective, they clearly showed that once you're with the right people in your life, you feel alive again.

Whewwwww!

Wayne and Braam weren't finished. They had another anvil on the way.

At the end of the video, there's a scene where all of the campers say their goodbyes and hug each other before walking off into the horizon. One of the campers, a young teenage girl, stops and slowly turns around. She looks directly into the camera with an expressionless face. The camera switches to Azora for a few more lyrics, and then goes back to the girl. This time, ever so subtly, she smiles.

Dammit, they got me again. My eyes welled up. Anyone who had ever been alone in the mainstream could easily relate.

The next day it was time for the campers to go home. I picked up Darren shortly before noon. What followed was the shortest conversation we'd ever had.

"You want to go to MSSD now?"

"Yep."

"You got it."

The madness in the mainstream was finally over.

Also from the author of
Madness in the Mainstream:

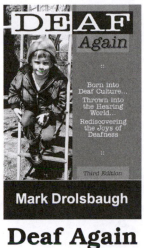

Deaf Again

Join Mark Drolsbaugh in his fascinating journey from hearing toddler... to hard of hearing child... to deaf adolescent... and ultimately, to culturally Deaf adult. Having the strange distinction of being born into a deaf family and being told to stay away from the deaf community, Drolsbaugh takes the unbeaten path and goes on a zany, lifelong search... to become Deaf Again.

"This is an excellent and highly readable autobiography that will soon find a place in the classics of deaf writing."
    -- The Forest Bookshop
    Gloucestershire, England

"This book is a MUST read for any hearing parent whose child has been identified with a hearing loss."
    --MaryAnne Kowalczyk
    The Communication Connection
    Manahawkin, New Jersey

For more information, visit our web site at:
www.handwavepublications.com

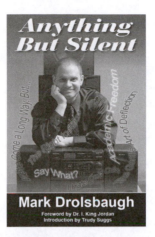

Anything But Silent

Anything But Silent is a compilation of the most thought-provoking articles by renowned deaf writer Mark Drolsbaugh. With a perfect blend of humor and insight, Drolsbaugh tackles some of the most profound topics in deafness: deaf/hearing relationships, the rift between American Sign Language and English, the hidden world of the hard of hearing, oppression in politics and education, idiosyncrasies of the deaf and hearing, embarrassing moments, and much more. *Anything But Silent* offers a deaf perspective rarely seen in print — bringing knowing smiles to those familiar with the deaf community and enlightening those who are new to it.

"Mark Drolsbaugh is a writer with this amazing ability, magical even, to tell a story that hits home every time. Whether it's about the frustrations or awesome joys unique to the world of deafness and sign language, he pulls in his readers for an eye-opening experience. You're in for a real treat so sit down, get comfortable, and enjoy the ride!"
— Marvin Miller, Executive Director
The Laurent Institute

"Anything But Silent so beautifully captures the essence of the deaf community. It's an empowering and entertaining collection of writing that truly shows what it means to be deaf. I know this to be true as a hearing mom having raised two deaf children of my own."
— Carol Finkle, Founder/Executive Director
Creative Access

For more information, visit our web site at:
www.handwavepublications.com

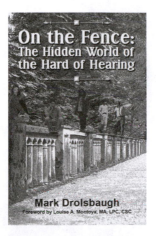

On the Fence:
The Hidden World of the Hard of Hearing

Mark Drolsbaugh
Foreword by Louise A. Montoya, MA, LPC, CSC

On the Fence:
The Hidden World of the Hard of Hearing

This is a book that delivers a rare inside look at a virtually invisible population. Deaf writer Mark Drolsbaugh, who grew up hard of hearing, has assembled a group of thirty-seven talented writers who share their remarkable stories and poems. Together, they shed light on the hard of hearing experience and what it means to be on the fence— hovering somewhere in between the deaf and hearing worlds.

Topics include:
- Communication methods and preferences
- The importance of belonging
- Bluffing one's way through work, school, and family events
- The two words hard of hearing people absolutely hate to hear
- Hard of hearing CODAs (Children of Deaf Adults)
- Tips and strategies for effective communication
- A faith healing experience gone awry
- Stories from hard of hearing grade school, high school, and college students
- Deaf and late-deafened people who also spent time as "fencers"
- Turning adversity into triumph

Stereotypes are smashed as each writer shares a unique perspective that may radically differ from the others. You'll find an American Sign Language advocate in one chapter and a cochlear implant advocate in the next— anything goes! But don't let the diversity fool you; while no one is exactly the same, deep down we all share one common goal. Find it in *On the Fence: The Hidden World of the Hard of Hearing.*

For more information, visit our web site at:
www.handwavepublications.com